9/25/21   1-00

1—

HILLABY'S WORLD

By the same author

WITHIN THE STREAMS
JOURNEY THROUGH BRITAIN
JOURNEY THROUGH EUROPE
JOURNEY TO THE JADE SEA
JOURNEY THROUGH LOVE
JOURNEY HOME
JOHN HILLABY'S YORKSHIRE
JOHN HILLABY'S LONDON
JOURNEY TO THE GODS

HILLABY'S WORLD

Adventures across three continents

BY
JOHN HILLABY

SINCLAIR-STEVENSON

The publishers and the author are extremely grateful to Constable and Co. Ltd, which first published the extracts taken from previous titles by John Hillaby and revised and rewritten by him for this volume, and to the *Daily Telegraph*, which first published *Kasbah of the Kingmakers*.

British Library Cataloguing in Publication Data
A CIP catalogue record for this book is available from the British Library.

ISBN: 1 85619 166 4

Typeset by Rowland Phototypesetting Limited
Bury St Edmunds, Suffolk

Printed and bound in Great Britain by
Clays Ltd, St Ives plc

I am a part of all that I have met;
Yet all experience is an arch wherethro'
Gleams that untravell'd world, whose margin fades
Forever and forever when I move.

Contents

Land of Feast and Famine 9

The Mother of Rivers *(Congo)* 37

Journey through Britain 59

Journey to the Jade Sea *(Kenya, etc.)* 99

Tales from the Dales 147

Telouet – Kasbah of the Kingmakers *(Morocco)* 173

Mountains of the Moon *(Zaire, etc.)* 183

Acknowledgements and picture credits 233

Index 235

Marrakesh

Land of Feast and Famine

To reach the Barrens, the most godforsaken landscape I have ever seen, I flew for what seemed uncountable days and nights, first across the steep Atlantic stream and then halfway towards the Rockies. Somewhere over Labrador at half-past one in the morning – dawn at that time of the year – the pilots throttled down the four fans at the front of the old Britannia, which began to whistle as it nosed down towards the vast field alongside Goose Bay.

The outlook above and below: mushy grey. An overnight thaw. Good for the countless thousands of wild geese and smaller fowl feeding on the ground, but downright perilous for the pilots of big ships. Two small birds sucked into the air intakes have been known to down a Flying Fortress. We circled as the radio operator spoke to ground control.

He leaned forward and said, 'They'll shift 'em in less than five minutes.'

What happened could not have been more effective had it been a volley of shotgun fire. That huge array of wild fowl flapped like lines of washing in a high wind before they made off west towards their breeding grounds around Hudson Bay. Not a bird in sight as we touched down, except two or three peregrines or maybe goshawks hacking their prey to pieces. Professional falconers had trained them as bird scarers.

We scrambled out, yawning, stretching, looking at the lemon-pale sun behind an inverted ocean of clouds. The plane had been towed off for refuelling and an overhaul. Glorious silence. To hell with the promised breakfast of ham, eggs and buckeye beans. I wanted to walk.

'Not here, sir,' said a military sentry carrying something like a Kalashnikov. Peevishly I tailed after the crowd.

Three hours later, another plane bound for Ottawa trundled down a runway bordered by acres of wild plants which were vaguely familiar, some of them, such as the reddish-orange hawkweed, fairly rare in Britain. Accidentally imported aliens often run riot in a distant country where there is little or no competition from similar species or those that prey on them such as insect larvae. The classic example is the well-known Scottish thistle.

9

In the early part of the nineteenth century the infamous Gordons, the rich earls of Sutherland, quadrupled their fortunes by setting fire to the homes of their established tenants, who were reluctant to make way for sheep. This was the first act in the dreadful history of the Highland evictions. Hounded out of their homes, deprived of their livelihoods, lucky to escape with a few of their possessions, the Scottish cattlemen, especially those in Argyll, Ross, Cromarty and Sutherland, emigrated in their thousands. Thus began the Highland occupation of Nova Scotia and Labrador, where the Scots felt at home among acid soils, conifers, lakes and gaunt landscapes. Among them was a young Presbyterian clergyman from Kinlochewe – name unknown, but still referred to today in the records of ecology as 'son of auld Tammie' – who, despite early hardship and deprivation, had managed to make a good living from land near Goose Bay flying field, where we took off at midday.

In addition to good hard-worked land and a shieling or two, young Tam inherited a thistledown mattress which, for sentimental regard for the old folks, he kept in a loft until rodents and porcupines gnawed into it; he then threw it on to the communal dump, meaning to set fire to it one day.

Imagine his surprise when, on returning to his father's old place after a year or two, his neighbours congratulated him on his family's insight in managing to introduce their beloved emblem, the Scottish thistle. They were less pleased later when the plant all but covered some hundreds of acres. Too late one season they tried to scythe it down by a communal effort, but succeeded only in releasing more billions of seeds. Thistles across parts of the east coast of Labrador resembled heather on a grouse moor in September.

The imported pest was gradually brought under control, but as we took off from Goose Bay I looked with the interest of a naturalist at the few plants which still survive there, the relics of a century-old lesson in basic ecology. What else can one hope to find on long flights?

Until the advent of hyper-powered aircraft, a journey used to be a simple and intelligible matter of going somewhere for a change, and for the sake of seeing something different on the way. Daniel Boorstin, the American author and sociologist, points out that one of the subtle confusions, perhaps one of the great losses of modern life, is that we no longer have this refuge. As there comes to be less and less difference between the time it takes to reach one place rather than another, space shrinks and all but disappears. The world looks very much the same from a modern hotel, a car on a motorway, a seat on a jet plane or the deck of an ocean liner. We are moving towards Instant Travel. Nowadays, says Boorstin, it costs more and takes greater ingenuity, imagination and enterprise to work out and endure travel risks than it once

took to avoid them. Almost as much effort goes into planning an off-beat route as into surviving it. *Days without darkness*

In Ottawa I had been given a signed three-star pass which meant that I could whistle up any small government plane from Saskatchewan to the Arctic Circle. In the hotel bedroom that night I read and re-read the official card as if I'd won a football pool. At long last I could plan as I'd never been able to plan before. The next morning, as he shook hands with me before I stepped down into the moored float-plane, the minister's side-kick, a genial fellow, suggested that to get the feel of the outbacks I should take a day or two off in their Algonquin Park, where, as he put it, 'the trout are as long as your arm'.

The four-seater Otter with a canoe closely strapped over our heads barked like a dog as it leapt into the air. By keeping to the wide Ottawa River until we reached the rapids around Allumette Island we flew at about three or four hundred feet, then due west, climbing gradually above a pearl-pale mist. In that spring-warm air the noble stand of eastern white oak, red pine and black and shag bark, which is a sort of

Uranium City

hickory, were breathing heavily. I couldn't put a name to most of them, except the birch and the oak in their generality, but the ranger, a fellow passenger, could. He had graduated in commercial forestry and held strong views about what the giant paper corporations were up to.

In the grip of convection currents the plane bucked amiably like a seaside donkey released from tedious winter quarters and I felt much the same myself. *Au revoir ennui!*

Graham Greene once wrote that the books we read in youth influence us much more than any amount of religious instruction, and among my bed-siders had been Jack London's *Call of the Wild* and Conrad in the Congo. All high adventure. We skimmed down on some lake, name forgotten, tied up against a row of log cabins equipped with just about everything and settled down to days of luxury.

The Algonquin is roughly sixty miles square, and a permanent staff keep their eyes on elk, moose, bears, wolves, lesser beasts and visitors, who soon get some idea of what woodcraft and conservation is all about: an orderly intermixture of relationships under constant surveillance for management purposes. Here I fished, followed forest trails, saw beavers at work, moose with calf, a porcupine or two and birds I had never heard of. Jake the ranger, my guide, came from the famous Laurentides National Park in Quebec.

Half an hour before dusk, when 'skeeters' drove us inside around the wood stove, we got down to some essentials, including a few shots of the local tipple, Jack Daniels.

The question of what I'd come out there for was brushed off easily by claiming the curiosity of a radio and newspaper correspondent. Up to that point I hadn't realised the significance of admitting that I was staying for a few days in Uranium City, a few miles from where they mined vast amounts of the basic stuff of atomic bombs. Apparently the American press hadn't been allowed to poke around the place, but on the strength of a British passport and a pass signed by Lester Pearson, when he was Minister of Mines and Natural Resources, I could travel wherever I cared to.

With my credentials established, Jake unrolled a large-scale map and he and the pilot argued amiably about where I might see most by float-plane and river steamer over a period of about six weeks. My imagination racing in top gear at the mere sound of the place names, I grunted and nodded with assumed complacency: Reindeer Lake, Gold-fields, Cree Falls, Lake Athabasca, Yellowknife, Blackfoot Creek, Dog-rib Settlement and the Great Bear Lake on the Arctic Circle.

'Where you starting from?'

'Saskatoon,' I said. 'Don Lawson, who runs the Zoology Department, is an old friend of mine. We met several times in Europe. His students are doing a research project on Lac laRonge, wherever that is.'

'Just south of Churchill River, a training ground for smoke jumpers. They're fellers who are parachuted out of planes to put out forest fires. One helluva job. You wouldn't get me into it for a thousand bucks a week. I'm too fond of my wife and kids.'

The moon rose. A whippoorwill, a sort of cuckoo, proclaimed its name as precisely as a peewit of our northern moors. Behind it, a wolf howled, softly at first but when others joined in with mounting intensity, the soloist became the leader of a pitch-perfect concerto of exquisite beauty. Never before had I heard such an impressive chorus. I held my hand up until the sound died down, slowly.

Jake looked at me sympathetically and smiled. 'That's Charlie's lot,' he said. 'He's just telling us they're around. There's another pack about twenty miles away. Unless two or three bitches come on heat at the same time they next to never mix. They know each other's territory. One sniff at the wrong sort of piss and they're up and away.'

'What happens if they get too close?'

'We bang on the garbage cans or fire the twelve bore into the trees and they get the message. We know most of them by sight. Charlie's got part of his tail missing and the favourite bitch has a bare patch on her shoulder; somebody else probably tried to muscle in.'

'How big are the packs?'

'We don't know the other lot as well as these since we're in a no-go area for tourists, but I'd say fifteen or twenty a side.'

'What do they feed on mostly?'

'White-tailed deer. There are times when I wish to God we'd got more wolves. You can't grow a damned thing around here unless you fence it off.'

Before we took to our bunks he reminded me to bring my jacket in lest the porcupines got at it. I told him the story of auld Tammie's thistledown mattress, which I suspect he'd heard before. But he wasn't surprised about the porcupines. He reckoned they were more destructive than raccoons. They had gnawed away at his canoe paddles, his leather gloves and once the crotch of his spare breeches. As he called them sweat pigs the attraction is probably perspiration, perhaps for its salt content. I dozed off happily, listening to whippoorwills and bush crickets and wondering how on earth porcupines mate.

Within a few days, another plane from Saskatoon settled on to the two-hundred-mile length of Lake Athabasca with the grace of a gull. We taxied towards the shack town of Uranium City where about four hundred skin traders, prospectors and hard-rock miners were hell-bent on getting thoroughly plastered whenever they'd a few dollars to spare. If they went flat bust as happened from time to time they could generally lean on the Hudson Bay store for some ready at fifteen per cent.

Kurt Larsen, a bull-necked Swede who ran the only hotel and bar in North Saskatchewan, took one look at my pass and told me to put on the bill whatever I wanted, including drinks and birds.

'In Uranium City,' he said, 'a man's as good as his credit. Marie will bring your gear up in a couple of minutes. Go take a look at your room at the top of the stairs. It's the best in the house.'

With only a small battered case, a rucksack and a heavy tape-recorder I said I'd handle them myself. He looked at the machine with admiration. 'God! That's the biggest geigy I've ever seen.'

Within a few minutes of my putting on a clean shirt and pants somebody tapped on my door, gently, and walked straight in.

Enter the Madonna of the sleeping-car, Indian style. Even today I've

Thistledown

rarely if ever seen a more beautiful young girl. Exquisitely combed long black hair. Dark eyes to match. Delicate both in profile and full face. She wore a soft leather jacket and skirt, thonged and fringed.

'Marie Bastien,' she murmured and brushed something invisible off my left shoulder. 'A beautiful shirt,' she said, fondling it. And me.

A life-long friend of mine once said we'd talked ourselves out of more beds than ever we'd made use of. It happened again that afternoon. She didn't play hard to get. To my embarrassment, under guise of sorting out washing and putting away the few spare clothes I carried, she gently pursued me around the room. I told her I was very tired. She smiled and pointed to the bed. In some detail I explained how the tape-recorder worked. She didn't seem particularly interested. Fortunately, at the end of the corridor somebody called out my name, loudly. I shouted back and in walked a man in smart dungarees.

'Glad to meet you, John,' he said. 'Welcome to Uranium City. I'm Larry McClean, assistant manager of Eldorado, Nesbit-Labine Mines. I've got a message for you.' He saw the girl in the lavatory and said something sharply in Athabascan Cree which I guessed, rightly, meant 'Fuck off quick'.

'For Christ's sake don't go fooling around with Kurt's whores.

They're all clapped to hell. Listen. We've had a radio call from the Mines and Natural Resources. They say you can go down Eldorado UC5, the deepest we're working right now, but they ask you to wire anything you write about production to be put through to Ottawa before you send it to the *Times*, just to be on the safe side. Don't worry, you and I will be scrambling around together, and I know just what you can and what you can't write. How about coming across to my place for supper? I'll pick you up here in a couple of hours. Some silly bastard thinks he's into a bonanza so there won't be anyone standing up straight here after nine o'clock.'

After four or five days making tape-recordings I began to get something of the pattern of life in Uranium City. All outdoor activities were strictly conditioned by 'skeeter hours'. Between six o'clock and half-past eight in the evening and two and half-past five in the morning the mosquitos arose in clouds, intent on sucking blood. The centre of infestation was the 'slew', a mid-town pond which couldn't be drained, at least not easily, as a spring sprang from a marsh some twenty or thirty feet below the sediment line.

The citizenry could have used soluble pesticides or oiled the surface, which would have put paid to the flies' larvae in a matter of hours but made for problems with public utilities in a community where tolerably fresh drinking water cost over a dollar a barrel. Why they didn't tap it from the vast depths of the lake I never discovered. The stock answer was they reckoned it was cheaper to purify it on the spot.

Uranium City had only been in existence for about a couple of years when I arrived there. Most of the shacks had been dragged around the ice on the lake from the abandoned community of Goldfields a few miles to the west. Those that had survived the haulage were being fired at the rate or two or three a month.

'To what end?' I asked Kurt.

'Insurance,' he said. 'Everything in this town burns well and the volunteer fire brigade charges over the going rate for water.' He reckoned there was one man behind a systematic scheme of arson, working on a percentage basis, but apparently even the Mounties didn't know which one.

Among those whose homes were reduced to charcoal was Betsy, a large self-possessed blonde who ran not so much a residence as a newly varnished house with three girls close to the Company Store. After a convivial drink or two in the hotel I thought, wrongly, that I'd got to know her well enough to put a straight question. As far as she knew, I asked her, was there anybody in town who had it in for her?

Betsy looked first at my collar-button microphone and then at me.

'Young man,' she said, 'don't you go asking me any fool questions. My business is men with money to spend, fast.'

According to Doc McDougal who, Kurt told me, hadn't been cold sober for three years, those who should have known better than to be out and about during skeeter hours were part-time hunters and prospectors. Speaking with some authority he put it down to booze. They usually carried a bottle for medical reasons. As he put it, 'If they think they've struck it rich the stupid bastards knock off a skinful and lose their way by leaving their tents in the hope of shooting a deer.'

If they got lost without even the protection of smoke from wood fires they were at extreme risk, not only from dense clouds of skeeters but also from minute black flies known to the Indians as *No-see-ums*. Men who got bushed had been known to tear their clothes off and, partly blinded, wade up to their chins in lakes. The doc had seen their bloated bodies when they brought them in days later.

No-see-ums, he assured me, could kill wood buffalo. Apparently most big game such as elk, caribou and moose were protected by thick fur, but wood buffalo were only partly acclimatised to jack-pine scrub. They were refugees from their natural habitat, the declining forests of noble conifers on the edge of the Great Plains. Their genitals were almost naked, an easy source of an unprotected meal for black flies. Agonised by ferocious attacks, the buffaloes' last resort was to run their underparts against rocks which, if unduly sharp, occasionally lacerated them to the point where they bled to death.

Although there wasn't even a dirt road beyond a radius of seven miles to the north of the Great Lake, the local population was redoubled on alternate Fridays when taxis and truckloads of hard-rock men from half a dozen syndicates swarmed in with a fortnight's pay in their pockets, intent on raising merry hell.

A racial intermix, many of their forebears had come, originally, from Scotland, Cornwall, Poland, Czechoslovakia, Spain and Bolivia. 'Once a miner, always a miner.' They drank, played poker and blackjack, and sold skins behind the Company's back – technically illegal since they were probably in debt to those long-sighted usurers. No matter. They sang songs that might have been heard in the golden days of the Yukon River:

> *All the biscuits as hard as brass*
> *And the beef as salty as Lot's wife's ass.*

On the nights when the Mounties patrolled Main Street, Kurt hung up a notice which said in letters three inches high that anyone who hit a man would be barred for at least a month; those who took pot-shots at bottles on the bar would be charged five times the value of the liquor spilt, but if anyone bust a window or one of his huge fly screens he wouldn't be seen there again for at least a year. Inga, his attractive wife, kept a Black Book. They took skeeters seriously in Uranium City.

The base of the lift shafts at Eldorado – over six hundred feet in depth – gave a fair impression of Dante's Inferno. We sweated profusely. Welders at work on the scaffolding raised cascades of sparks. Hammer blows on rivets were deafening. The sound echoed from a network of low galleries. Bare to the waist, wearing hard hats and boots with steel toecaps, we stumbled forward, crouching, sometimes crawling, through tunnels of rock lit by points of light like glow-worms. Larry carried my tape-recorder wrapped up in a sack.

At intervals of about two hundred yards we entered 'dog holes', elongated caves where men were using pneumatic drills. We hurried through with our hands over our ear pads. It took us longer than I now care to think about to reach a chain of power-hauled trucks on two sets of rails.

In a relatively quiet length Larry told me we'd been through a drift of rich dirt. There were a dozen or more ahead.

Suddenly lights began to flicker and hooters blared, mournfully, like a distant herd of cattle. Larry glanced at his watch. He touched a button and the trucks stopped.

'In five minutes they're going to start blasting, but not in this length,' he said. 'Turn round and put your hands over your eyes. There may be some dust flying around.'

I couldn't distinguish the initial explosions from a volley of echoes which seemed to gain in intensity amid that labyrinth of galleries but by counting the gusts of air which swept over us Larry said that five shots had been fired.

'Had enough?' he asked. 'It'll be much like this until they start hauling the stuff out in a couple of hours.'

The 'stuff' is pitchblende or uranite consisting mainly of uranium oxide, mother-lode of the two most deadly isotopes known to mankind, U235 and U233. Apart from nearby rival combines, Eldorado was milling something around a thousand tons per day.

After being crushed and subjected to complex chemical treatment the 'hot' slurry was flown off in canisters resembling milk churns to where nuclear technologists refined the stuff to the required molecular level.

To make just one atomic bomb it was necessary to blast out the potentially explosive isotopes of enough rock, pitchblende or uranite equivalent to building a small Egyptian pyramid. There isn't *an* atomic

secret. It's the thousand or more technological discoveries about such *Chips schoolhouse*
things as radioactive widths based on Einstein's theory that Energy (E)
equals Mass (M) times the speed of light (C) squared.

As we bumped back to Kurt's place I thought – but didn't say – that
in my opinion the world would have been an infinitely better place if
scientists had never discovered the potentialities of uranium.

Apart from trivial detail about the chemical composition of the hot
stuff, Ottawa passed on my piece about Eldorado to the *New York Times*
virtually untouched.

About an hour after dinner each night we heard the call of wolves
but too far away to make a good recording without a sensitive parabolic
reflector around the microphone. How could we get closer to the pack?
I asked Jock Mercredi, a half-Indian skin trader at the Hudson Bay
store.

'Easy,' said that fruity-voiced man. 'Come with us tomorrow night
when we peg out husky bitches on heat; their erotic cries will bring
them many eager lovers. A cross-bred wolf-dog is a *vairy* good sledge-
team leader.'

It came out that way. A spectacular performance.

19

The scene: a clearing among Jack-pine scrub above Lake Athabasca. The time: near midnight, with the sky ablaze with the shimmering blue, green and purple of the Northern Lights, aurora borealis. Everything we touched produced a shower of sparks in that log cabin. I worried about the tubes, the thermionic valves in the heavy recorder. We were swathed in mosquito netting.

Five or six huskies were staked out at intervals of about fifty yards. Even before the pegs were hammered down they announced their sexual condition by copious urination and heart-throbbing calls.

In complete silence, like a commando operation or a spoonful of mercury splashed on corrugated cardboard, the wolves slipped through the trees, a pack of maybe a dozen animals.

They assembled around their leader, the king dog. He tiptoed forward towards the nearest excited bitch, but stopped on his haunches to announce his seigneurial rights with a howl that began slowly and rose and fell within an octave. Apart from much vigorous tail-wagging the pack was quiet and still.

As far as I can recall the scene – I carried both a stop-watch and field glasses in addition to my notebook and tape-recorder – he covered the bitch in two minutes sixteen seconds. This done, he rolled aside, licked himself, stood up and howled again, this time more softly and in a different key.

At this, what must have been the best lupine choral society around Uranium City responded with a group howl before they set about pleasuring their chosen partners with remarkable orderliness. Those low in the pecking order hung about obediently as if in a nicely conducted bordello.

That concerto between a king dog and his pack eventually became the overture and leitmotif of a BBC series called 'Men of the North', for which I brought in the late Alan Civil, that maestro of the French horn, to analyse the calls in musical terminology.

He said the howls of the pack leader, the virtuoso, contained 'at least five harmonics either a little above or a little below an octave'. He thought it interesting 'that although most if not all the wolves started *pianissimo*, only the pack leader had the ability to rise to *messa di voce* apparently on one breath before sliding down a bit incoherently to where he had started within the tonic'. This threw most of us completely but Alan, with his horn and his superb vocal duets with the recordings played at half speed, stole that programme.

Mercredi and a young anthropologist, Vic Valentine, whom I met the previous day, assured me that unless they were suffering from rabies, wolves had never been known to attack man. They rarely fought seriously among themselves. It looked as if dominance, an inbuilt sense of social order, had been ritualised by their musical howls.

At the store, Mercredi told me he'd heard that a band of Redmen at an encampment down the lake were 'going to light a fire'. They were 'Chips' (Chipewyans), one of the last tribes to dance before they set off to slaughter caribou. They chased them on dog-drawn sledges and drove them over cliffs.

'Their priest, Father Leo, isn't all that keen on the old Indian stuff,' Mercredi said. 'And he's having real trouble with the Chips this year. The Bounty Boat [Indian Agency] isn't due in for at least a week, maybe more, and they're as hungry as hell. Only the chief accountant – who's a mean bastard – knows what they owe the store in the way of credit. Right now there's only peanuts in trapping. Ermine and muskrat have dropped to a dollar a skin; fisher and beaver to twenty, marten to fifteen. I recall it near eighty.'

There spoke a professional skin trader accustomed to his employer's knowledge of the intricate cyclic nature of the abundance and scarcity of valuable animals in that land of feast and famine. Basically it stands four-square on fairly regular fluctuations in the winter climate: deep snow one year, slightly less deep the next one and so on over a period of six or seven years until the cycle starts again with early snow falls, a late thaw and a relatively short summer.

Among carnivores nothing lives alone. They are entirely dependent upon their prey, mostly herbivores which, in turn, are dependent upon snow-free vegetation or limited periods of hibernation in warm tunnels below the snow which, if it's a really heavy fall, may force them to the surface. Arctic foxes, for example, feed almost exclusively on rat-like lemmings which during good, that is to say moderately warm, winters breed at a prodigious rate until they are obliged to migrate in countless millions – hence the well-known plagues of lemmings – or remain where they were born and quickly starve to death. In the high latitudes the climate is Nature's pruning hook. As a theoretical ecologist, a reporter of other people's scientific work, I had travelled a long way to witness and to find out something about the inter-relationship between Man and animals for myself.

As a store keeper and trader Mercredi spoke fluent Chipewyan. I tracked him down to Kurt's saloon where, half drunk, he was doing his best to argue logically with Vic Valentine, a sober young man who was assembling a generalised dictionary of what he called the Athabascan linguistic group: Chips, Yellow Knives, the tribe that used to specialise in copper weapons and utensils, the Dogribs, Slavies, Hares and Tanaki from the Barrens and northernmost lakes above the Arctic Circle. Could either of them act as interpreter and get me to Stony Rapids in time to see the great fire and the caribou dance? I asked.

Vic said he couldn't. He was flying back to Saskatoon the next day. But maybe he could talk Jock into a deal. He closed one eye and spoke to him in a slow mixture of French and Chip.

Answer: yes, if I could give him a hand with his canoe to avoid the falls on a short cut. It would cost me two bottles of hard stuff, half of it on a handshake. The deal was done and Jock lurched towards the bar. Vic and I talked for hours. He had seen caribou at a range of fifty yards.

The local Redmen, he told me, were at the end of their tether. They were wildly improvident on a class system based simply on 'those that have' and 'those that have almost nothing'. They had no sense of time; no set meal times. They gorged themselves and then went without food until they began to feel ravenously hungry again. If they were employed as casual labourers they disappeared as soon as they got their first week's pay. 'Why should I work? I didn't need the money.'

Each year they were visited by the local Superintendent of the Indian Agency, who turned up by boat and gave every tribesman five dollars, some ammunition (shells) and meagre emergency supplies, including Wood-buffalo meat which they promptly scoffed. He hoped to get them a freezer to see them through the summer.

They were casual trappers and deprived hunters. The great herds of caribou had scattered except for relatively few in the Barrens, 'the Place of the Little Sticks'; some among the wooded belts of 'the Dwellers among the Shivering Aspens' and a scattering preyed on by the tribes

Chips chase caribou

First casualty disemboweled

around Hudson Bay, 'the People under the Rising Sun', mostly Cree.

Together Mercredi and I, looking like evil spirits in our skeeter veils, trailed through the scrub amid the calls of distant wolves which he assured me were just curious. Light a fire, he said, and they turned up to see who was around.

'How come you got the name Mercredi?' I asked. 'Were you born on a Wednesday?' Puzzled look. I explained. Laughter.

'Not Mercredi. My mother a Chip squaw; father Scottish man, McReady.'

The serpentine track on to which I shouldn't have ventured on my own wove in and out of stands of conifers thicker than I'd experienced in Scandinavia or Germany. No sound of wolves; almost total silence. Probably the blind wilderness in the sense of seemingly endless forest must always be more fearful than the open bush, the plain, even the desert, for the plain and the desert allow for exertion, for the resolute march that serves to dampen doubts and uncertainties and the almost irrepressible voice that whispers, 'You are lost, you are lost.' The forest is the nightmare of the half-shadows where the compass is of no avail.

Jock had no need of one. He loped ahead. He seemed at home amongst dense trees. Not surprising, this, in the child of a Chip – 'The People of the Pointed Skins', meaning the caribou hides once used for their conical teepees among the Little Sticks.

From the forest we emerged into Jack-pine scrub, bright with the shrubs and flowers of the tundra, bilberry and bog myrtle, stonecrop and saxifrage, pink, yellow and purple. Far ahead, close to the river we were heading for, came a noise uncommonly like a dog fight heard at a distance.

'Wolves?' I asked.

Jock shook his head and bent down as if patting a small dog. Young bears? No! He bared his teeth and growled ferociously. He muttered an Indian word unknown to me, but clearly they were animals best left to themselves. I discovered later, when I saw a pile of furs in the Company store, that they were wolverines or gluttons, ferocious brutes about the size of a badger which in family packs have been known to drive cougars off their prey.

The river looked placid enough at a point where Jock knew there to be a birchbark canoe, common property, tethered to a tree but, as he explained, there were two places where we should have to drag it out for portage before we reached the encampment at Stony Rapids. I clutched my tape-recorder. He said, 'Don't wobble if you want to keep your ass dry,' and pushed off, paddling deep.

Within two hours of midnight we reached the first of the rapids. The sky became blood red and the foaming river took on the colour of the sky. It might have been an outpouring of lava.

In that Wagnerian light we hauled out the canoe, no heavier than a folded ironing board for two men, but unwieldy even on a well-trampled but narrow portage trail.

'How do you handle this alone?' I asked him.

'*Facilement*,' he said, handing me the paddle and a small parcel wrapped in brown paper, which from the shape and gurgle contained a bottle.

'*Comme ça*,' he said, stretching his arm across the central strut and lifting it as any mother might a child out of a pram. We stumbled on.

At the second portage east of Woodcock Falls Jock heard an explosive cough repeated about a hundred yards ahead and put his forefinger across his lips. In a clearing, silhouetted against the sky, a huge cat crouched on one of the upper boughs of a White spruce. It saw us and snarled before leaping away. An Arctic lynx. The remains of a hare fell from the tree.

Soon afterwards we heard the wail of husky dogs and the sound of children's laughter. They were playing football with a pine cone tied up in a bit of caribou skin. What they shouted to each other in their own language was incomprehensible, but the laughter was that of children anywhere.

Half an hour before midnight the mission bell began to clang and at each stroke it wiped out more and more of the laughter, until there was no sound except the sad wailing of dogs. A meagre congregation of about fifteen, mostly women, dutifully filed in for Mass. Father Leo had struck a bargain with his flock. If they insisted on dancing that night, he had told them, they had to go to church before they lit their fire. To the evident surprise of the priest, we joined the service shortly before the General Confession, in which the responses were intoned slowly in a curious mixture of Chipewyan and Latin. It sounded like the growling of dogs.

Father Leo, a little old man with a beard, came from Neerharen in southern Belgium. He greeted us warmly and invited us to supper. I said we should be glad to join him later on but first I had an important message for his chief, a man with the rather improbable name of Louis Chicken. I didn't admit it was from the manager of the local Company store who was getting worried about his credit. He wanted more skins, soon.

This clearly put the priest aback. He did his best to postpone the meeting until the next day and I soon understood why. The Redmen were intent on a saturnalia.

We could see the fire half a mile away. It blazed like a haystack. Like most poverty-stricken people the Chips were wildly improvident. They burned everything they could lay their hands on.

Louis had a well-worn face, deeply furrowed and, for an Indian –

Caribou spotted

who tend for good reasons to be a melancholic people – a ready smile. His two counsellors, Pierre Laban and Germain Crow, could have stood in for Rosencrantz and Guildenstern in that band, the former with forehead villainous-low and no visible teeth, the latter bearing facial evidence of an encounter with an unfriendly bear. They sat on the floor and rarely spoke. Drunk, I'm pretty sure, and looked as if they'd been that way for days.

Jock, my interpreter, said the local tipple was moose milk, concocted, as I understood it, from boiled and lightly fermented raisins laced with methylated spirits. After introducing me to Louis he handed over his gift parcel, a bottle of liquor which was promptly opened and also, to my surprise, two steel combs.

26

'What did you tell him about me?'

'You come from far far 'way across water which no man can drink but in your land there is a little snow and many trees. That's how you put it in Chip.'

After a few words with several of the band about hunting – 'very bad, caribou not come near the lake that year' – I asked Jock when the dancing would start.

'It depends on Louis.'

Holding the bottle by the neck that cheerful fellow sat in the official chair with his hair down and unbraided. To his evident satisfaction he was being deloused with the combs by two young squaws, 'his friends', the only women in that huge hut. Outside the fire still blazed furiously.

Without rising from his seat Louis took a swig from his bottle; the others tapped a wooden keg into nipperkins mostly made of tarnished copper. He sang something slowly, pausing for what I took to be short ritualistic responses.

'What's he saying?'

Fight for mates

27

'I have much difficulty in telling this in your language *mais j'essayerai*. "Our land is our land though white man everywhere take it from us. This night we ask help from those who came before us in days when together we had plenty of meat from caribou, *n'deni*, *n'deni*. Now we believe *n'deni* go only into the *mistik – ka – ma – ta koo*, the Barrens."'

When the liquor took over, the braves, mostly dressed in tattered jeans, started to bash their tom-toms, made of caribou skin tightly stretched over a frame of bent willow. To that accompaniment they danced around the remains of the fire, howling wild monotonous songs virtually indistinguishable one from another: *di-dee-didee, di-dee-deee, di-diddy-dee*: bang! bang! It ended temporarily in a remarkably realistic imitation of a chorus of wolves – their totem animal, Valentine the anthropologist had told me. For this sequence Louis Chicken took over the role of the king dog.

Next came a Ghost Dance in which they dragged a leg as if they were lame while their women folk threw pieces of pemmican and brick tea into the fire to reassure their ancestors they had not been forgotten. Suddenly Louis Chicken held up his arms for silence and began to sing in a deep, guttural voice against a pattering beat from the drums. Quite unexpectedly he threw his voice up into a falsetto wail. He asked help from the sky in what Jock called a Bridge Song, a pathway between earth and heaven. I listened fascinated and recorded much of what I heard. As Jock was developing what his Scottish father would have called a taste for the stuff, I walked back to Father Leo's place alone.

He looked crestfallen, down at soul. It was *soo* bad, he said, that I should have *soo* wrong impression of his people. He allowed them to dance twice a year and he intended to find out where the liquor came from.

A message for me from Saskatoon. At about midday a big flying boat would touch down nearby. Malignant pneumonia and smallpox had broken out among Indians around the great lakes to the north, Great Slave and Great Bear on the Arctic Circle. They were sending a medical team. I could join them if I cared to.

We got down to an early-morning (2.30 a.m.) supper: pemmican, sweet corn, potatoes, with two generous glasses of communion wine. Father Leo's last words to me the next day before Jock paddled me out to the flying boat were: 'It was at Neerharen in Belgium that I learnt to pray. I shall go back in two years. Perhaps one day you will visit my little town.'

Thanking him I said, politely, perhaps I should, not knowing that eventually I should spend an erotic night there.

On the way out to the limits of the wooded country the pilot pointed down to where a large herd of caribou fled from the scream of our twin engines. Running alongside them were small packs of wolves like *Author with admirer*

29

Grey wolf country

Caribou on migration

Cossacks on the flanks of Napoleon's army retreating from Moscow.   *Cheerful Chips*

With props feathering our aerial boat floated down to one of the biggest outlets of Great Bear Lake, the Mackenzie. Scores of Redmen lined the shore and not a word was spoken except by a counsellor of the Dogribs whose chief they had buried the previous week. The place reeked of death. They had taken to cremating bodies in deep stone-lined pits marked by a palisade of pointed poles that touched at the apex little fingers in prayer or the frames of their teepees.

One of our medicos, Jim, gave me two shots in the arm and advised me not to touch anyone who had not been examined. We – that is, Harry, a sort of odd-job man with an outboard dinghy and a portable radio, and I – stayed in the vicinity of Fort Rae whilst the others flew round the lake on a macabre survey and treatment course. God knows how many might have died or nearly died but for their intervention.

As we cruised up and down an extensive bay, parties of Redmen came down to their fishing platforms and waved. They needed help, urgently. For the same reason plumes of smoke came from their encampment inland.

With considerable knowledge of the region, Harry told me that the Indians next to never washed themselves thoroughly. At most they might squirt a little water on their hands and faces. Their summer locations were surrounded by piles of offal and garbage; food for their emaciated sledge dogs. Instead of sweeping up and keeping their premises clean, they simply moved on somewhere else. It was easier. They were mostly on the move. Harry thought lack of hygiene lay at the heart of their periodic epidemics. In this he was largely wrong. As with syphilis, smallpox and certain strains of pneumonia, these diseases were brought in by the White man.

The severe cases of confluent smallpox were hideous to look at. Faces blood raw; noses and lips barely distinguishable.

Our flying boat returned twice with encouraging news. Although severe, the outbreaks were localised. With the co-operation of a few chiefs and their *shamans*, the medicos thought the diseases might be contained. They had erected a modern dispensary. In addition to more medicaments being needed, many bands were desperately hungry. It had been a year of famine; the fur cycle was at an all-time low. What were left of the once vast herds of caribou had split up in an easterly direction towards the Barrens and Hudson Bay. The Dogribs and Hares wanted to follow them, but that would reopen the old tribal wars and the medical team had no powers to advise them.

They had radioed Saskatchewan, which in turn got in touch with Ottawa. As far as they knew, they were due to pick up the Superintendent of the Indian Agency from Athabasca or Great Slave the following day, a momentous day that ended in a gaudy night.

Harry and I went off in our outboard. Trailing a spinner I fished and caught more huge trout in half an hour than I had a conscience to kill; on a large island Harry knocked off several Arctic hares with a light rifle.

'What's going to happen to those Indians?' I asked.

'Fuck all. If this lot moved east they'd clash with the Cree. They hate the Cree. Many bands still won't speak to them. The Crees were the first to get guns from the Hudson Bay Company who run the skin trade. With those guns they blasted their way west. Most of the Indians are on their way out. It's just a matter of trying to keep the survivors quiet.'

Somewhere close to skeeter time we cruised back to the moored flying boat to find that ashore the powwow, under the direction of a most

affluent-looking Indian, the Agency Superintendent, had got down to
dealing out shells, supplies and the customary five dollars and answer-
ing a long list of complaints. Only the trivialities received much in the
way of attention. One man wanted a new spring for his artificial foot,
another had run out of salt and chewing tobacco. Dead serious questions
about why they couldn't buy liquor or pursue the caribou for hundreds
of miles were brushed aside by the ridiculous suggestion that they
should send a deputation to Ottawa.

New dispensary

Overhead that night the Northern Lights set fire to the sky. The
silhouette was extraordinarily clear. Against the golden centre the cloud
changed colour in an infinite variety of red-violet, lilac-pink, red and
orange tones. Up towards the zenith and downwards in a southerly
direction its contours appeared as if blown away by the wind and
surrounded by a fan-shaped turquoise green, gold-rimmed field it slowly
vanished into the air. I thought of Louis Chicken and his Bridge Songs
appealing to the sky for help.

Is this what Chief Seattle of the Duwarmish, inheritors of the huge
dripping evergreens of the Pacific Northwest, asked over a hundred
years ago? As he put it: 'How can you buy or sell the sky, the warmth

33

Tepee skeleton

of the land? The idea is strange to us. We do not own the freshness of *Redmen's chief*
the air or the sparkle of water. How can you buy them from us? . . . *administrator*
We know that the White man does not understand our way.'

By deploying every dirty sub-legal trick in the book, the giant hydro-
electric-dam builders, their satellite logging corporations and poisonous
smoke emitters in their jackal capacity of cheap power absorbers were
forcing the Redmen to sell their land and work for them amid the ruins
of once glorious country.

Let Chief Seattle speak again: 'When the last Redman has vanished
from the earth, and the memory is only the shadow of a cloud moving
across the prairie, these shores and forests will still hold the spirits of
my people, for they love the earth as the newborn loves its mother's
heartbeat. . . . One thing we know, our God is the same. The earth is
precious to him.

'Even the White man cannot escape our common destiny.'

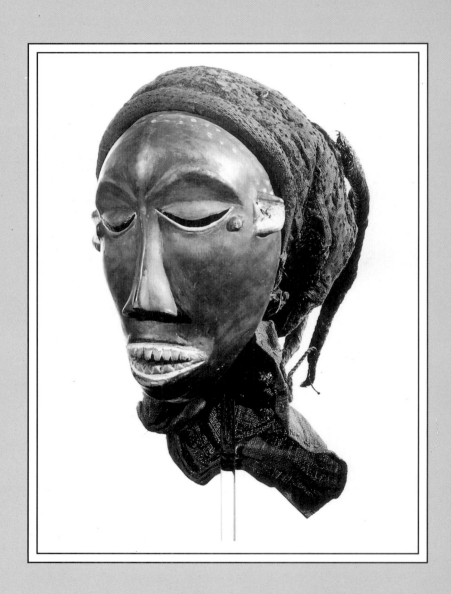

THE MOTHER OF RIVERS

A T A TIME when almost everyone in the Western world seems to be flying somewhere or other, the passenger in the next seat is rarely a complete surprise. We've become accustomed to the irrepressible chatter-mongers, the home-coming packaged tourers with their packs of family prints, the salesmen of just about everything including salvation. Until Peter Pavel from Prague boarded the plane from Brussels at Iraklion *en route* for Khartoum and what used to be called Stanleyville, I thought I'd seen them all – which is one on the nose for heavy generalisations. From his gestures, his delicate features and his varnished fingernails, I assumed within half an hour of swopping platitudes that he was homosexual and then, quite by accident, discovered what could never have been guessed.

He was, I learnt, a salesman for the worldwide Bata Shoe Corporation. Because he spoke several European languages in addition to Swahili and, as he put it, a smattering of Arabic, his paymasters had put him in charge of an enormous domain, the whole of the old Belgian Congo from Kinshasa, the Leopoldville of earlier years, to the borders of Uganda and Tanzania. He'd been at it for most of his working life. Just the man I wanted to talk to. In the rack above my head was a valise containing maps and a detailed itinerary for a two or three months' tour of the Congo drawn up by the generalissimo of their Overseas Parks Department in Belgium. Most of the regions meant no more to me that what I'd read about in London.

Before I could say more, an air hostess turned up with a variety of drinks with the compliments of SABENA. We chose brandy and soda and touched glasses. 'To us,' I said, 'and all who love us. By the way, do you happen to be married?' It slipped out. I heard myself saying it, but he smiled and answered in such a matter-of-fact voice that for a minute or two I thought he was pulling my leg.

'You will understand,' he said, 'that this is not a subject I usually say much about, but between Stanleyville and the coast I have eight wives and am now on my way to recruit another one in Khartoum, where I hope to develop some new business. What do you say in England? That trade follows the flag? Well, I have a flag of my own.'

'Surely you mean eight girl friends?'

'Not at all. Marriage is a serious matter. Wives can be honourably bought, that is with the approval of their fathers, and their fathers are therefore my fathers-in-law, my customers and my local agents.'

Under cover of admiring the cognac and comparing it with Metaxas I wondered how on earth I could ask the fellow how much he'd spent on his harem in terms of bride-price and maintenance. How often did he visit his flock and what were they up to when he wasn't there? Peter, I'm pretty sure, sensed this and changed the subject.

'What are you up to in the Congo?' he asked.

A radio and newspaper correspondent, I told him. The Belgians had commissioned me to bring them in some publicity to attract tourists, but with the exception of the Parc Albert most of the reserves were used only for research purposes. Their scientists didn't like tourists around the place. But everything was changing. The new socialistic government in Belgium needed money to manage nearly all the reserves and bring in more and more tourists. Among other things, they hoped I might be able to suggest where they ought to build rest houses and game-viewing platforms. I had yet to admit to Peter or anyone else that this was the first time I had set foot in Africa.

'Where are you based?' he asked.

'Two or three places around Lake Kivu, wherever that is.'

'Marvellous place not far from their eastern border. A small lake. High up. About fifteen hundred metres. Next to no change in the temperature day or night. The Belgians are spending a lot of money on what they're calling the Playground of Central Africa. I know just where they'll be taking you. Pygmies in the Ituri forest. Gorillas, too, and active volcanoes. One of them blew its top about six months ago. Then there are the drummers and dancers in Rwanda nearby.'

'You seem to be an authority on the region. Have you a wife there?'

'Yes,' he said, with what appeared to be a touch of pride. 'But not among the people you are likely to meet, *les colons*, the rich bourgeoisie. I should not fit in with what my colleague in Athens calls *philotoma* which is close to the Orientals' notion of "face". I sell large numbers of cheap sandals to the natives, often in remote villages. Bata's expensive shoes with high heels are for sale in fashionable shops. Around Kivu look for them in Goma and Kisenyi. Tell them who you are and please mention my name. Mutual *philotoma*, eh?' Impossible not to warm towards the most original salesman I am ever likely to meet.

Over a little more brandy I learned that he steamed up and down what he called the Mother of Rivers about half a dozen times a year, disembarking, staying for a few days, unloading part of his stock with the headmen, his fathers-in-law and salesmen on a percentage basis. Was Bata aware of what he was up to?

River market

39

In an international business, he said, a man was as good as his sales record and they were about to make him a director. In any case he hoped to retire in two or three years. But not under the flag of the Belgians – 'the most boring people on earth'. What did it matter? By that time the Belgians would probably have been kicked out. Had I ever heard of the *Kitiwala*?

'You mean the secret independence movement?' He nodded.

Several people in Brussels had told me about it, I said. But always with an air of assurance. They reckoned they'd got it under control. At the least sign of an insurrection they flew in troops from half a dozen airfields and shot it out, mercilessly. Apparently they'd got native spies in all the critical areas, especially around Coquilhatville.

Possibly because he realised he was talking to a reporter, Peter merely shrugged his shoulders and said, diplomatically, that as he travelled about he had heard quite a lot, but it was almost impossible to distinguish between facts and gossip. As for himself, he was a salesman, an internationalist, and hoped there'd be no trouble, certainly not before he left the country for good.

Near midnight, within half an hour's whistle down to Khartoum, the C 26 began to buck like a horse and in his best captain-speak the pilot assured us it was just what he had expected: the deserts of mid-Sudan were being thrashed by the *haboob*, a wind which, as we discovered when we bumped to a standstill, sounded like the noise of escaping steam. The hot blast might have come from a furnace. We were cooped up until the jet engines were muffled against the high-powered blasts of sand which could ground any sort of unprotected plane.

In the bar of the transit lounge, jet-black Abyssinnian waiters in starch-white gowns moved with the quiet dignity of seminarists, a ritual ruined by a fat American woman who, dissatisfied with whatever she'd ordered, waddled up to the bar to complain. Predictably Peter and I were within arm's reach of the dispensary.

My eyes were focused on the suspended bottles of sticky liquors which were festooned with interesting moths, flying ants, cicadas, praying mantids and other invertebrates I couldn't put a name to. The fat woman saw them and screamed. I thought, perhaps I hoped, she was going to faint. One of the Abyssinians glided towards what looked like bell-ropes. He pulled them. Curtains parted and an immense window swung open in that air-conditioned lounge. Within minutes, attracted by the bright light, in swept four or five large bats with mustard-coloured wings. They hovered over the lines of bottles and rid them of every insect with the efficiency of vacuum cleaners.

Peter tried to persuade me to stay in Khartoum for a day or two, offering tours of the black brothels in Malatesta and the huge *sukh* in nearby Omdurman, reputedly the biggest in Africa, where we should be able to see veiled female slaves up for auction. Impossible, I told him. Parcs Nationaux were sending a private plane to link up with my arrival in Stan the next day. How could I get in touch with him up and down sections of the great river?

'Wherever the big boats pull in,' he said, 'you will find the *chef de port* in the office of OTRACO, Office d'exploitation des Transports Coloniaux. Whatever you do, first shake hands with him, present him with my compliments and ask if he knows where I'm likely to be found. I think I know them all and they know me.'

Gongs chimed twice for an announcement. We were due to take off in half an hour. Before I walked out into the embarkation lounge I turned again and waved to Peter Pavel on his way to meet the next of his bartered brides.

Until the pilot announced that we were coming down from 25,000 feet, the great river appeared no wider than the Thames. As we were landing it looked like an inland sea of kidney soup. Formalities at Stanleyville were trivial, courtesies memorable, but there was no air-conditioning where I waited to be picked up. The air, inside and out, felt as if you could push it with your hand. The conditioner, I was told, had gone on the blink. I reflected on the events of the last thirty-six hours, and made some notes in my diary:

> Am lolling back over a sun-downer in a miniature Garden of Eden around the SABENA guest house. Unexpectedly luxurious. A snap of the fingers and Figaro in a red fez materialises out of apparently nowhere with an outsized iced drink. Reflect. somewhat piously, that I'm among strangers in the tropics and not in our place at St James's Street and sip it, slowly, combing the lambent air, trying to absorb the sights and sounds of birds and insects such as I have never seen before. Impossible to distinguish between the squeaks, trills and chirrups of hummingbird-like Nectarinids hovering seemingly motionless and a host of finches, weavers and crickets.

Figaro came in again apologetically with a message from the manager's office. He'd been phoned by my first host, Camille Donis, Chief Conservateur of Kivu, to say that their flying field of lava dust had been flooded but he'll try to get a small plane out the next morning. Will they please look after me at the Park's expense.

After centuries of sleep (nearly ten hours) the manager recommended a visit to the *chutes* (the Stanley cataracts) where the mainstream drops forty feet in a series of lava steps and becomes the Lualaba river. Locked at on a simple map the tributaries of the Congo are infinitely more intricate than the veins of an autumn leaf. An oafish Belgian doorman began to bawl out the young black driver, a law student with whom I'd already struck a more than reasonable hourly contract. I told the doorman to shut up and got in. Peter the polygamist had warned me that the less intelligent the White man is the more stupid he thinks the Blacks are.

Charlie Mutara and I got on fine. A tall Nilo-Hamite from Rwanda, he spoke near-perfect English and asked me to make 'correct small bits of talk said wrong'. What were his hobbies, his interests outside his professional studies? Tribalism and geology. His father, a surveyor, had a Belgian doctorate.

We could hear the roar of white water when we got near the biggest cataract out of several overhung by scaffolding about twenty feet in height, made from tree trunks woven together by lianas and telephone wires. It looked like an enormous spider's web. Somewhere in it, I felt, there should be a giant spider, perhaps Archaeo-arachnida, about the size of a dinner plate, which lived in the age of dinosaurs. Partly submerged at the foot of most of the uprights were fish traps – conical in shape, about six feet in length, made out of wickerwork, their mouths gaping upstream.

Nobody about. Charlie glanced at his watch. The traps would be emptied in about half an hour, he said. It happened twice a day in the rainy season. During the dry months they rebuilt the whole structure by hammering more poles into cracks between the rocks. The fury of

The river

Ritual masks

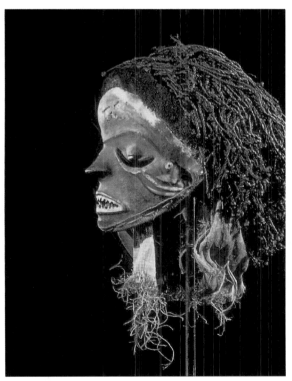 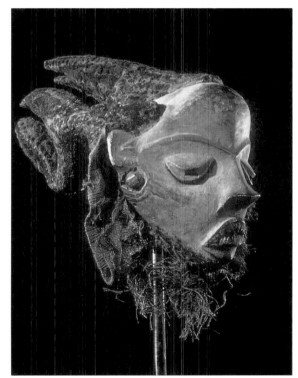

the water was caused not only by the staircase but by the narrowing of the mainstream to about 500 yards in width.

Right on cue both banks were enlivened by thirty or more fishermen in small dugouts and family boats paddled as if their life and livelihood depended on it – which they did. If they overturned downstream below the traps it didn't much matter – they could flap ashore. But upstream there was more than a chance they would be impaled on the sharp fangs of the wickerwork.

Everybody made it to the nearest of the uprights where Wagenia fishermen moored their boats and shinned up to the crude platform at the top of the poles. There, with the agility of acrobats, they jumped about, selecting woven ropes to haul up their fish traps. Sometimes they leaned over, heads downwards, to get a better purchase with their legs crossed. Among them were three or four all but naked young women who shrieked with laughter at some pantomime of their own and seemed by far the most athletic of them all. Their wet black skins, their firm upright breasts looked beautiful.

I asked who were selected for such a highly skilled job. Charlie shook his head. He didn't think anyone outside this branch of the tribe knew much about their social life. Lower down the river family group of Wagenia fishermen merely used long nets suspended between floats in calm water. These were specialists who lived in a village of their own and shared their co-operative profits according to what each individual did. The girls, he said, would marry rich husbands who probably owned two or three boats.

They were beginning to come ashore, again fighting the water. I looked at their catch. Very few could I recognise apart from perch, carp and hideous-looking catfish with flat heads and prehensile whiskers. Among them were some intriguing fish with iridescent bodies like mackerel with huge upward-pointing pectoral fins. Surely they were flying fish?

Charlie spoke in a variant of Swahili to one of the Wagenia, who grinned, flapped his arms and gave a pretty good imitation of them leaping out of the cataracts and skimming over the surface. He smacked his lips noisily. Very good to eat, he said. Inedible species were thrown back into the water where they were pounced on by birds, especially fish eagles and ospreys.

Within an hour the stage was empty, the performance over; the players had walked off, lugging their hard-won rewards, but the cataract continued to roar. Not monotonically. It had some sub-aquatic rhythm of its own, audible at the surface. A rise and fall in baritone voice. I couldn't find out what it was, but told Charlie I didn't think that as a ritualistic way of earning a living gracefully I had ever seen anything more impressive.

On the way back we settled round a collection of dilapidated old cars, especially rusty Cadillacs, once I suppose a dump which now served as a village for Blacks who looked far from distressed. Beyond them we came across an encampment of battered dugouts loosely covered with canvas. In a sandy clearing between habitations a circle of children danced around three albino kids of about their own age. Charlie said they were blind, and they were plagued by flies which they seemed too indolent, too woebegone to resist.

My first reaction was one of indignation. Weren't they being taunted by the others? Not a bit of it, he said, they were being cheered up, entertained by those who gently pulled their ears or patted their little bare white heads as they danced. Charlie had a few wrapped-up sweets in the car which he distributed, to everyone's delight.

Where did these cheerful ragamuffins come from? I asked. Those in the bust-up cars were respectable odd-jobbers, most Wagenia and Babali, he said, but the dugout people were a highly specialised branch of the Lokele who still practised 'message drumming'.

Back in the museum at Stanleyville that afternoon I learnt that the tribe's craftsmen made two kinds of drums, or, more accurately, wooden gongs hewn out of hard logs up to four feet in length and two feet in diameter, traversed by a deep slit that narrows towards one end. When struck by the drummers' iron-wood sticks the narrow portion emitted a high-pitched *tock*, 'the female voice', while the more open portion, 'the male voice', sounded like *toonk*, as if an empty biscuit tin had been struck by the palm of a hand. By a rapid series of *tocks* and *toonks* with intervals of about a second between the 'words', messages could be sent up and down the river for about five or six miles under favourable – that is, mist-free – conditions, and much further when repeated by intermediaries.

They opened up their nightly inter-communication system with something very roughly equivalent to the old Morse-key operators' call sign, which can be phoneticised as 'diddy-dee-dah-dee', meaning 'please come in if you are receiving me'. Whereas Samuel Morse demonstrated to the US Congress the feasibility of sending a message ('What hath God wrought . . .') over a wire from Washington to Baltimore in 1844, the explorer Henry Morton Stanley heard the Lokele drum a mere thirty years later and there's reason to think that it's been used on the great river for over a thousand years.

The *tocks* and *toonks* are not symbolic like dots and dashes. They phoneticise actual words by means of lengthy phrases that minimise but don't actually eliminate homonyms, that is, words that sound

Man bathing

almost alike, such as poll and pole. Most African languages are tonal, so that intonation can give two completely different meanings to what might appear to the uninitiated to be the same word. Thus *teesakā* means swamp but *teesaká* means a promise. This can be difficult if not embarrassing in Kingwana, the language of the river, where, if you want to borrow two donkeys (*punda*) from someone, it might easily be mistaken for his testicles (*punbu*).

To get round these complications in low notes and high notes (*tock* and *toonk*), quite simple words are tapped out on drums in lengthy explanatory phrases. For example, testicles are 'what you make babies with' and the White man is referred to as 'the spirit of the forest', the person who suddenly appears where he's not expected, while the cockerel or rooster, one of his favourite meals, is referred to as as 'the big bird (*N'dege m'kubwa*) which shouts *oo-ko, oo-ko*'.

Journeys usually begin far more slowly than they end. As I sat down in the guest-house that night to transcribe hastily scribbled notes into a leather-bound diary, it became apparent that the warming-up process was reversed on this trip. I had almost too much to write about and it was midnight before I went to bed.

There are those who emerge from deep sleep in a very slow manner. My response to an unfamiliar sound is a split-second sleep/awake reflex. Tropical forests are never silent during the night. Incalculable hosts of insects are forever at work reducing vegetation to the basic elements of fresh growth, but even above that chatter, which didn't disturb my

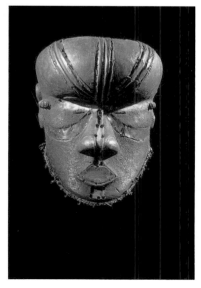  

Ceremonial masks

sleep, I awoke immediately to the tappity-tappity sound of Lokele drums *staccatissimo*. Time: three thirty. I felt as if I were eavesdropping on a private conversation. A glance at my compass showed that the loudest were probably coming from that sorry collection of dugouts below the cataracts, while more faintly, almost if it were an echo, came the response from the nearest village downstream, a place called Yangambi about five miles to the east. What were they telling each other? The museum curator compared it to a local paper giving news of births, marriages and deaths, all of them occasions for boozy parties where the prime tipple was banana beer (*pombi*), often spiked with pot.

At eight o'clock the house phone rang. Manager speaking. Air controller had told him a light aircraft from the Parks Department was asking permission to land to pick me up for Kivu. As their flight paths were overloaded, could I be ready to leave in half an hour?

Activity everywhere on the strips. Apart from the Comets, the flagships of British Overseas, the big planes were recognisable only from their national colours. They came and went. An air hostess pointed out my Cessna buzzing around like a tired bee. I thought it diplomatic not to ask her about a large Belgian troop carrier with its tail protruding from a badly camouflaged hangar, but remembered what Peter, he of the bartered brides, had told me about Kitiwala, the insurrection movement.

M. Maurice Ory, a young *conservateur* with a curly upturned moustache and all the manners of a former RAF fighter pilot, managed to land in a distant corner of the airfield. He stood with his back to the four-seater, trying to disguise what he felt about being left aloft with next to no gas in his tank.

·'*Enchanté, M'sieu*. Welcome to the London Airport of the equator. You had a good flight in? Good show! Pop in. Got to fill her up somewhere. I'll ask Control.'

Within a quarter of an hour we were heading for Bukavu on the lake where, he said, they were getting a bit anxious about him. Nevertheless, to give me a fish eagle's view of the cataracts, he swung in low over the Wagenia's nets and clung to the great east-flowing river which, swollen by more tributaries, got progressively wider upstream until it was, he told me, about ten miles from bank to bank. What happened to the water when it reached Stanleyville? He didn't know. He shrugged his shoulders and said maybe it became *pombi*.

We were still flying low over yet another tributary, perhaps the Ituri, the forest kingdom of the pygmies. Dense clumps of trees were interspersed with prairie or bush, the pastures of the hippo and buffalo.

48

'What's on the programme at Bukavu?' I asked him.

'You're going to meet the principal *conservateurs*, your hosts. They're in charge of our four national *parcs*. There'll also be some famous scientists, including Dieter Backhaus of Frankfurt Zoo and two American professors. Quite a conjugation of talent, eh?'

Nothing in Switzerland could rival the Royal Residence Hotel for conspicuous opulence. Set on the top of a peninsula of manicured palm trees between two bays of the lake, it was wreathed in the scarlet and white bracts of poinsettias.

About a dozen of us lolled on settees around our principal host, M. Camille Donis of the nearby, largest and most sophisticated park, the famous Albert, which covered over two million acres.

As we'd arrived late it was necessary to undergo brief introductions all round, together with handshakes which in Belgium are obsessional and conducted within strict rules of precedence. Whoever is the first person to extend his right hand establishes precisely where the shakee stands in the estimation of the shaker. As they'd already gone through the routine with the other outsiders, Dieter Backhaus and white-haired Professor Richard Foster Flint of Yale, probably the best-known glaciologist in the United States, and an equally distinguished American anthropologist, M. J. Herskovitz, it remained only for me to be introduced extravagantly as a man who'd come along to visit their reserve and do my best to give them some publicity.

Fortunately I knew quite a lot about those reserves (on paper), because for several years the Parks Department in Brussels had been sending me copies of all their reports for retransmission to the press and radio.

After two hours of technicalities our host suggested that before we sat down to lunch we might care to take a drink with Madame Celestine, his wife, in an adjacent suite. As an old hand in the business I'd been to many junkets of this kind, which usually range from unruly affairs put on by admen, publishers and traders for their clients to intimate ceremonials among friends with intentions in common. This was of the latter kind.

The Belgian *conservateurs* dutifully lined up in order of precedence to pay their respects to their hostess, an uncommonly handsome woman with a wry smile, her mouth turning up slightly at the corners. I knew Dick Flint slightly from his visits to London. Under cover of examining a huge bowl of orchids at the back of the suite we exchanged pleasantries, awaiting our turn in the queue. Predictably Backhaus and Herskovitz got in first.

Wagenia fishing nets

Mme Celestine spotted an irregularity. '*Messieurs*,' she called, 'I don't think I've had the privilege of meeting either of you before.' Mildly reproved, we slunk forward while the rest waited. And listened.

To me she held out two fingers at shoulder height which I kissed, lightly, episcopal fashion. She smiled. '*M'sieur* John,' she said, 'welcome to our little colony. Last night your Uncle Victor phoned us up from Brussels and, thinking you were with us at home, sent you his warm regards.'

Rarely have I received more undeserved respect among strangers. A *nephew* of their supremo? I still wonder whether the ploy was unpremeditated or whether this intelligent woman had made the best of a mischievous opportunity. Only she and her husband knew that two or three years earlier I had met Professor Victor van Straelen, both the president and the chairman of just about everything biological in Belgium from their National Museum to the Congo Parks Department. We had corresponded with each other. He invariably addressed me as '*Cher Monsieur* John'. He'd invited me to Brussels to discuss this trip and at a small party at his home I had referred to him to a mutual acquaintance, slightly facetiously, as '*mon oncle*'. Fortunately it appeared to amuse him hugely.

In addition to the *conservateurs* at Bukavu that morning I was introduced by my graceful hostess to two other men, amusing and outstanding characters, my friends and guides on many exciting occasions. As Mme Celestine put it: '*Monsieur* John, you will be our guest for as long as you would care to stay at our home in Rumangabo, but, alas, we are obliged to make an official tour for perhaps two weeks with His Excellency the Governor. In the meantime we are leaving you in good hands. Here is our old friend Gaston, M. le Baron Gaston de Witte, an expert in many zoological matters, especially those I am not too fond of myself, snakes and other reptiles, and this is our famous young geologist and mountaineer, Jean de Heinzelin.'

These two professionals were wholly unlike each other. Gaston was in his seventies, crop-headed, short, fat and proud of his Flemish ancestry. Before he retired to the Congo with his life-long if rather thick-witted manservant, Pango, he had held several consular appointments in various parts of the world where, I soon learned, he spent most of his time collecting and writing scientific papers about reptiles, and drinking prodigious quantities of Dutch gin.

By contrast, the aesthetic, good-looking de Heinzelin, a Frenchman with a small château in the Alpes-Maritimes, was as slender as a gazelle. After gaining his doctorate in Paris and studying further at Louvain, he had already spent two years in the Congo, studying active volcanoes and the structure of the Ruwenzori, the Mountains of the Moon. The next morning, accompanied by Gaston and Pango, I set off in their Land-rover for my first experience of big game (and snakes) at close quarters.

After three weeks spent mostly in the bush, that's to say largely among grassland interspersed with umbrella-shaped euphorbia trees, I became no more surprised by the sight of groups of elephants, rhinos, buffaloes, hippos, warthogs, lions, baboons, gazelles, and occasionally zebras, giraffes and hyenas, than I should have been by the sight of vehicles on a busy day in Oxford Street. Not that the animals stood still when they heard, saw or got wind of our noisy, bouncy Land Rover. In Gaston's expressive phrase (he spoke flawless English), they exhibited a 'positive p.o.q. reaction' – that is, as he put it, 'They pissed off quick.' He fully understood their varying flight distances, that point at which a surprised animal runs away or – very rarely in open country – adopts an aggressive posture ready to attack.

Gaston deeply respected rhinos and buffaloes. He had been charged many times and never ventured out on foot without a high-speed 30 06 over his shoulder. In the Land Rover he was a different man. If he spotted groups of animals through glasses, at ranges of up to half a mile, he never drove directly towards them. He began a slow, encircling movement, closing the diameter each time round, perhaps three or four times in all, until we were within sixty or seventy yards of the centre of the group. Then he slackened speed, but he always kept going, very slowly. Animals are scared of inanimate alien objects.

By these manoeuvres we usually became part of the faunal scenery, together with cattle egrets, fidgety crowned cranes and flocks of wattle plover. I say usually because on one occasion Pango, unable to restrain his curiosity about a herd of peacefully grazing zebras, incautiously raised the back flap of the closed vehicle and they galloped off, barking like dogs and bumping into each other as they ran, with a few cow-like eland lumbering along behind them.

On another occasion we came across the heart-touching scene of a male rhino frustrated in his attempts at copulation through sheer impetuosity. In our own inexperienced youth hadn't we been in similar circumstances? Gaston explained that for complex gynaecological reasons the female rhino requires to be covered twice within a specific interval in order to be fruitfully fertilised. The conjugation is complicated even further by the fact that the penis of the male is everted, that is, except during an erection it points the wrong way, backwards not forwards, and in order to be mounted by her partner the female is obliged to lean forward and stretch out her back legs like a ramp up which he must laboriously climb. To put it plainly, he fell off the job three times; to judge from the position of his genitalia he had ejaculated and now lay on his side, presumably with a headache.

In between bird and big-game spotting Gaston poked into every hole and corner in pursuit of his favourite quarry, snakes and lizards. He spread canvas sheets underneath trees and ordered the reluctant Pango to climb up and shake the branches. In this way he picked up half a dozen ribbon snakes, bright green and about ten or twelve feet in length, two small horned vipers and a fair-sized puff adder, in addition to what he caught on the ground, sometimes yanking them out by their tails. All were meticulously sexed, measured, classified and some of the poisonous ones 'milked' for manufacturing antivenenes.

One of the most theatrical events of the day occurred right on cue just after lunch, when Gaston had been talking about mambas, both green and black, which he said were very dangerous. They were nimble creatures, too, in his opinion and one of the very few snakes likely to pursue and attack you. A big specimen had once chased him into his house and tried to get at him at the foot of the door, which he had slammed shut.

Leaving Pango to prepare a camping site, we set off in the Land Rover down a track in gallery forest. Tall trees, mixed on one side and mostly euphorbia on the other. Suddenly Gaston became excited. A large green mamba about ten feet in length swung towards us. The 'foot' of the snake, about three feet of it, was on the ground, acting as a vigorous propellant. At an angle of about forty-five degrees the rest of the creature thrashed purposively from side to side. It looked distinctly ominous, a film director's concept of a deadly serpent, which of course it was.

'Wind your window up!' shouted Gaston. 'It'll strike at anything.'

I quote from my diary:

Gaston swerved away, stopped and gave me the wheel and got out his bamboo pole with a wire noose at the point. 'Chase it,' he said. Nobbled it in second gear with the mamba going flat out, I suppose can't have been doing more than about five or six miles an hour. So much for the speed of deadly snakes. Gaston went through the usual routine with gloved hands and much wrestling and released the creature by shoving it foot by foot through the window opened about eight inches.

The following day we drove back in the dusk to Gaston's place in the Kagera Park near the common border between Congo, Uganda and Rwanda. Windscreen wipers working overtime to remove flattened insects. The air painfully thick with flying termites while overhead a rose-coloured glow like an immense chrysanthemum flickered in the western sky. Made by the reflection against clouds of a bowl of agitated lava in the crater of Nyiragongo (11,400 ft), one of a chain of eight volcanoes in the Virunga to the north east of Lake Kivu, the last remaining home of bands of mountain gorillas.

'You'll be up there with de Heinzelin in about two or three days,' Gaston said. 'Too high for me. My old ticker won't stand it.'

'How far up do you expect him to take me?'

'Right up to the rim,' he said, before adding – with a chuckle – 'probably at night. He goes up there regularly to see whether there's any danger of the lava vomiting over the top. It's blown up about twenty times since the first Europeans got there in 1822. It looks as if the present eruption is dying down.'

Gaston's well-appointed study was dominated on one side by the skin of an immense snake draped over the mantelpiece like a shawl and on the other by a striking, a positively frightening, native death mask that seemed to embody everything explored by what the French social anthropologist Lévy-Bruhl called the duality, the 'bi-presence' of the ever-dead with those still-alive. The dead lived in a world of their own. Natives understood it. We can only marvel at credulity beyond our comprehension. The mask haunted me whenever I sat in his lounge. As Gaston put it, he had 'acquired that curious object' from a missionary. That's where most of the masks had gone, he explained. Under guise of converting heathens to Christianity the missionaries swopped them for a box full of bibles and a few buckets full of maize meal. The masks were extremely valuable among dealers from New York to Brussels. Among the Holy Fathers I encountered on my way to the Ruwenzori I saw several of them and was taken aback on each occasion.

As for the skin of that snake draped over the mantelpiece it was a Rock python, fifteen feet in length. He grabbed it on Mt Elgon where it was 'somewhat lethargic'. It must have been caught in a fall of snow. He thought it was only a little short of the world record. 'I spotted it, curled up to keep warm. I kept an eye on it and sent Pango back to bring up eight strong men. We could have done with twelve. It slowly uncoiled. I tried to shove its head in a sack, but it knocked me over. Constrictors aren't venomous, but by God they can bite and once their jaws snap shut they don't let go. The men were just chucked about. Pango, unfortunately, was at the tail end where it had wrapped itself round his throat and shoulders, so there was only one thing to be done.' He picked up a carving knife from the table and went through a sawing motion.

'For most reptiles, especially the big ones, the tail is both a weapon and an additional leg. Marc Micha, who runs the Garamba Reserve up north near the Sudan border, once saw a crocodile kill a big rhino which was trying to swim across the Albert Nile. The croc seized it by one leg and dived repeatedly until it managed to anchor itself by its tail on something on the bottom of the river. In his report Micha said lots of blood and bits of flesh appeared on the surface which probably attracted other crocs. For a time the rhino appeared to be holding its own, but gradually it was pulled into deeper water where it was dragged beneath the surface.'

Pango knocked on the door and brought in a fine dish of roasted warthog surrounded by bean shoots. After he'd sharpened the carving knife, Gaston looked at him and pointed to the snake skin on the wall. Pango grinned, rubbed his throat and said, 'N'yoka n'kubwa sana sana.' It was certainly a very big snake.

After the meal with an abundance of wine – wardens are given a generous allowance for entertaining visitors – I asked him what he would have done with the constrictor if he hadn't been obliged to kill it.

'Given it a heavy shot of tranquilliser, examined it carefully and then let it go. Mind you, you've got to look after it until it becomes active again. If hyenas or some other predator had got at it when it was dopey they'd have polished it off. Army ants, too, might have done it in. They're one of the most formidable insects in Africa. They move about in millions. Micha's pony was left tethered in a railed-off paddock by some bloody fool of a boy. He came back to find it half eaten by rats but it was quite obvious that the ants had got in first.'

Traditional fishing method

54

'But how did they kill it?'

'Panic and suffocation. They attack through the mouth, nostrils and the rear end.'

Pango came back with a letter brought in by a runner from de Heinzelin. Gaston scanned it rapidly and told Pango to give the man something to eat. Then he could spend the night in the lines.

'How far has that man run today?' I asked.

Still reading the letter he said, 'About thirty miles if he's come from Bukavu. But hold on a minute. This is a bit complicated. Help yourself to the liquor.' He looked at his diary, made a few notes, put the letter down and sighed. 'God-damn Parks are always changing their minds. Now this is the new arrangement. Jean can't pick you up tomorrow. He's got to fly down to Leo with the Americans, Foster Flint and that irritable old fool Herskovitz to meet His Excellency and Camille Donis. But it'll only be for a few days.

'He says, "*Au diable avec l'administration! Disons quatre, cinq jours pour plus de sûreté. Moi, je vais voler à Bukavu et j'arriverai chez vous le quinze ou seize mai. Faites mes amitiés à Monsieur John. Il me semble que vous et lui, tous deux, avez un respect pour les propriétés pharmaceutiques du genièvre et du Scotch.*"'

He paused as he poured out another brandy. 'You are in for a long safari. Jean's going to take you from here to Butembo, where he's arranged to hire some porters for the scramble up to the rim of the volcano, Nyiragongo. Perhaps after that you'll go into the rain forest to see the pygmies at Epulu. I might come part way with you. We'll fix all that when he arrives.

'The big thing is the climb up into the Ruwenzori, the Mountains of the Moon. About four or five days up into the glaciers and snow. Watch out for the leopards among the giant heathers. They are nearly twice the size of those you'll see around here.'

In fact I did see them, and have no wish whatever to see them again, but that, as the princess said, is a tale for another occasion.

Elephant hunter

Journey Through Britain

SOMEWHERE UP IN the high forests between England and Wales I had been walking for hours and, not for the first time, I had lost my way. All tracks seemed to lead west when it was clear from map and compass that I should be heading north. Down in the valley an old man explained in elaborate detail how I'd strayed miles off course. In any case, he said, there wasn't much worth seeing even had I got to where I intended to spend the night. A thoroughly dispiriting old man. From time to time you meet them. I thanked him and began to move off.

'Where've you come from?' he asked. Not wishing to go into the history of a walk scarcely begun I named the last town I had passed through. But he wasn't to be put off that easily. He wanted to know how I had got *there*. With a touch of pride I said I had walked from Bristol. He looked adequately surprised. Had I started from Bristol?

'No,' I said. Truth must out. Why not relate all? I told him I'd walked from Cornwall. He looked astonished. For the first time in my life I felt pleased with myself.

'From Cornwall?' he said. 'Do you mean to tell me you've walked *all* the way here?'

I nodded. Shaking his head sadly, he said, 'Then all I can say is it's a pity you couldn't be doing something useful.'

You can't win. Go to the Arctic and the Congo and see hosts of wild animals and people say you were darned lucky to get the chance. They look like exotic stunts. They reckon it's just a matter of being able to raise the cash.

If, on the other hand, you decide, as I did, to walk across your own, your native land, they tell you it has been done many times before. Men have set off on foot, on bicycles, on tricycles. Somebody has even pushed a pram from Land's End to John o' Groats. But all that, of course, was done on the roads I tried to avoid.

For me the question wasn't whether it could be done, but whether I could do it at the age of fifty. I'm interested in biology and prehistory. They are, in fact, my business. For years I've had the notion of getting

Starting point

59

to feel the whole country in one brisk walk: mountains and moorlands, downlands and dales. Thick as it is with history and scenic contrast, Britain is just small enough to be walked across in the springtime. It seemed an attractive idea. There was challenge in the prospect. But to see the best of what's left I knew I should have to set off pretty soon. Each year the country, in every sense of the word, gets a bit smaller.

I set off with the intention of avoiding *all* roads. I meant to keep to cross-country tracks and footpaths all the way. In places this turned out to be practically impossible, for notwithstanding what's been written about the ancient byways, many of them are now hopelessly overgrown; others have been enclosed, ploughed up or deliberately obstructed in one way or another. As far as I know you can't get into the Midlands from the Welsh border or cross the Lowlands of Scotland without making use of country lanes, derelict railway tracks or, in places, the towpaths of old canals. I did my best to keep off the public arteries, but I sometimes got squeezed into the little capillaries of transport. Otherwise I kept to the out-of-the-way places, especially the highlands and moors.

From Land's End I followed the cliff-top paths of Cornwall for sixty or seventy miles and then struck east into Devon, crossing the centre of Dartmoor and reaching Bristol by way of the airy uplands of north Somerset. Then up the Wye Valley through the Forest of Dean, in places one of the most beautiful woodlands in Britain. A roundabout route through the Black Mountains, Shropshire and industrial Stafford-shire led me into Derbyshire and the foot of the Pennine Way. From there a high track along the spine of England extends north as far as the Scottish border. In the West Highlands I used what are called the drove roads, the old cattle tracks that wind through the deserted glens. In all I did about 1,100 miles in fifty-five walking days. It may have been much more; it may have been a little less. The calculation is based on map miles, which means I haven't taken into account innumerable forays in wrong directions.

As for trappings, I carried the basic minimum, including a tent that eliminated the need to look for lodgings at nightfall. This gives you a comforting sense of independence. I don't mean I'm overfond of the spartan life, certainly not for its own sake, and if I found a pub or a hotel at dusk I went in, gratefully. But I had no need to rely on static shelter.

At the beginning I managed to reduce clothing and the contents of a rucksack to about thirty-five pounds, adding comforts gradually to approximately twelve pounds over the initial burden.

Clothing is a simple matter. The trick is to wear as little as possible without becoming even a fraction too cold or too hot. The important thing is to feel comfortable throughout the whole day. I bought a light windproof anorak with a zip fastener down the front that could be easily adjusted. I zipped it up tightly when I set off in the morning and gradually increased aeration when I began to generate my own heat. On wet days I put on two pairs of skin-thin bits of protective clothing, made of artificial fibre, that were supposed to be waterproof. They gradually leaked. I never got very wet and certainly never wet *and* cold, which I had been told is fatal. For this reason I covered my lightweight cotton tent with an outer fly sheet made of Terylene that was wholly waterproof. When things got really bad, even during the day, I crawled inside. At night I slept in a bag quilted with what the salesman said were feathers from Chinese eider ducks. It felt like heaven, weighed three pounds and cost a lot of money.

Footwear is tricky. I treat my feet like premature twins. The moment I feel even a slight twinge of discomfort I stop and put it right. Most people advocate stout boots and thick socks. I know of nothing more uncomfortable. They give you a leaden, non-springy stride. You can't trot along in boots. I bought two pairs, broke them in and eventually threw them aside. After trying various kinds of shoes, I settled for an Italian pair with light, commando-type soles. They weighed about fifteen ounces each and, when oiled, fitted me like gloves. I had no trouble with shoes. Certainly not from blisters, although in the last stages of the journey some of my toenails dropped off. In places I went barefoot through bogs, and on warm days in deserted country, I sometimes wore only a pair of shorts.

MIST AND MEGALITH

I left at seven in the morning and have been asked to say that my wife was there to see me off. There isn't, in fact, much else that I can say. It was misty. I couldn't see much. I could hear nothing except the twittering of invisible larks. I felt dizzy, not from the height of the cliff-tops, nor from elation at the start. The feeling came from an unfamiliar breakfast of cold roast fowl and champagne. And that soon wore off.

Beyond the Land's End Hotel and the shacks of the trinket vendors, the path that should have led to the wild blue yonder became terribly overgrown. And it was much like that for most of the way. But that I didn't know as I dodged in and out of thickets of thorny gorse, looking for somewhere to squeeze through.

Here, as so often elsewhere, I can say relatively little about what preoccupied me most – that is an irrepressible, whirling stream of thoughts on which I became dependent since there was so little to look

First day out

Carn Gluze

at: a few undistinguished plants underfoot, a mad March or rather April hare that turned a half-somersault and ran away, thumping the ground, and above all a disconcerting silence.

Even the invisible larks had stopped twittering.

If the path disappeared entirely, as it seemed likely to, I decided from careful scrutiny of the map to strike across country to St Ives by way of Botallack, Carn Kenidjack, Carn Gluze and Woon Gumpus Common, names as strange as an incantation. I said them aloud and they sounded even stranger.

Much of the Cornish coastline is as desolate today as it was over 5,000 years ago when strange people arrived in boats with large leather sails. They were the tomb builders. They were peaceful men. They left no weapons behind. They came, it is thought, from the Mediterranean, perhaps Crete, although not, of course, in one stage. They established colonies on the way, where they practised the cult of the dead called the Megalithic. This is the religion of the people who built the quoits or stone graves found on both sides of the Irish Sea from Cornwall to the north west of Scotland. Like the ancient Egyptians, these priest-kings lived in order to die.

Megalithic means no more than a relationship to big stones. The term is confusing since it is used often to describe circles of upright stones, such as Stonehenge. Circles mark the site of seasonal rituals, not burials. They were built by the masons of a race of warriors who arrived after the priest-kings and probably overcame them. In Cornwall there are examples of both graves and stone circles.

Carn Gluze was excavated about a hundred years ago by a gang of miners directed by the famous Copeland Borlase, an antiquarian who opened up barrows with the confidence of a surgeon lancing a boil. Among what he describes as 'greasy mould', the remains of someone who died about the time of the Jewish exodus from Egypt, he found an amulet. Elsewhere his men discovered a bit of pottery and the bones of a lamb, perhaps a final sacrifice. Nothing else. Another barrows-despoiler had evidently got in before him.

Beyond the carn the moor is scarred by the ruins of innumerable barrows or earth mounds, each one an ancient grave. The majority were ransacked centuries ago by men in search of treasure. I intended to poke about among them myself but, to my dismay, after only five hours of walking my feet felt tired. I bathed them by treading barefoot in a refreshing patch of cold, wet grass. This done, I slept for twenty minutes, adjusted the pack and went on to more cairns and quoits.

Carn, like cairn, means a heap of rocks; a quoit by definition is a flat disc of stone or metal, a word also used to describe the roof of a Megalithic grave. There are more of these bits of prehistoric scaffolding around Woon Gumpus Common than anywhere else in Britain. To walk alone among them as I did on that first morning out of Land's End was a strange experience – strange and frustrating. Monuments are mute witnesses. Great circles are for miracles to happen in. They are not to be walked through with cold indifference.

At six o'clock that night, footsore and extremely dirty after a walk of twenty-four miles, I trudged down to St Ives. You can't wash in the town. The explanation is that if they installed public facilities they would be crowded out by the beatniks.

'A dirty lot,' said the car-park attendant, looking, I thought, at my knees. 'And no good for business,' added a man who sold candy floss at scandalous prices.

The picturesque little town harbours a few artists, but for the most part the local people live on boarding visitors and selling trinkets. The middle-aged and the elderly buy pictures of flaming sunsets, while the youth walk up and down looking for something to do. There is an undeclared state of war between the young and the old.

The patron of St Ives, the gentle St Ia, a virgin of noble Irish birth, is renowned as the saint who missed the boat. She and her companions agreed to set sail for Cornwall, but she came down to the shore too late. The galley had left. The early Christian scholar St Anselm says that in her grief she knelt down on the beach and prayed, long and earnestly, whereupon God wafted her across the Channel on a leaf, so that she reached her destination before the others. These Celtic stories come from medieval manuscripts, but they embody ideas of earlier times A common theme is of young people who came from across the sea and returned to the Isles of the Blessed before they grew too old. There are tales of islands of young girls; of the beautiful Deirdre, who beguiled a sailor into her boat simply that she might look once more upon the face of ardent youth.

In St Ives today the fishermen are less romantic. One told me he had seen a beatnik, a young girl, bathing naked at dusk. 'Not a bloody stitch on her,' he said, his voice rising in indignation. 'She got out and dried her hair on her pullover. I saw her, I tell you. Bold as brass. I should have liked to have given her a damned good hiding.'

Into West Barbary

I left St Ives at dawn, but not alone. The constable who woke me up insisted on accompanying me to the edge of the borough, explaining as we trudged along that the Vagrancy Act would apply equally forcibly in the next town. I tried to argue, pointing out that by camping on a vacant lot between the bathing huts and the esplanade I relieved pres-

sure on the official site at the top of the hill. The man poked around in my rucksack; he showed a certain amount of interest in my books on the birds of Britain and the archaeology of Cornwall, but conceded, reluctantly, that they were not evidence of evil intent.

All very humiliating, the more since I had planned to get up in a leisurely fashion, wash, feed and wave goodbye to the sleeping town. As it was I limped towards Carbis Bay, hungry and burning with indignation. I got a shred of satisfaction from recalling that in 1870 the vicar of St Ives confessed to the Reverend Francis Kilvert, the diarist, that the stink of fish in the town was sometimes so terrific it stopped the church clock.

In the eighteenth century Cornwall was known as West Barbary and so it looked to me, since it rained for two days and narrow lanes between hedges became rivulets; but that was naught compared with Dartmoor, where I splodged through a nine-tenths mist on a compass course and lost my way more times than I care to think about.

Dartmoor is a dome. From a distance it looks like an enormous teacake with a flat top and rounded sides. In the centre of the moor, as I had discovered, there is a great deal of moss that quickly becomes overloaded with water. This huge sponge is the source of about half a dozen big rivers and a lot of little streams. I had set off from the western rim of the dome, reached a point north of centre, and must have been about

Woon Gumpus

St Ives

66

halfway across the opposite side when I struck the wrong river. This, I knew, would add at least another five miles to the day's total. I reckoned that in all I had already done about twenty, but at least I knew where I was.

The day never really came to an end. It fizzled out, damply, like a squib that refused to burn. Stopping only to cheer myself up with a little Scotch and Dart water, I jogged on, mile after mile, playing the usual game of partly contrived thoughts. In time these become the iron rations of the intellect.

By five o'clock the river had become a noisy torrent, pouring over a series of waterfalls, hurrying along, too deep to be forded anywhere. At six o'clock I reached the point where it spilled over into another bog. With solid map references to work on I struck out for yet another tributary, the West Dart. More hut circles, rings and an avenue of stones. I scarcely gave them a glance. Wistman's Wood, a freak forest of dwarf oak trees which, I learned afterwards, is one of the most famous bits of woodland in Britain, hove up through the mist and disappeared again. I didn't stop. My mind wasn't on the wonders of nature.

At seven o'clock I got on to the road at Cherrybrook Farm to find that Chagford was still eight miles away. I shall say no more about the surrounds of that top-security gaol.

West Country Days

I walked up the banks of the flooded Exe, where I came across a philosophical road mender. We sat down together, the old man and I, and put the world to rights for about half an hour. Before we parted I asked him a few personal questions. Did he drink? As much as he could get, he said. But it didn't come easily these days, not at the price it was. Cider? I enquired. Not that stuff, he said. All right for young chaps, but it made him fart, went through like a dose of salts. He preferred beer. Where was he raised? He came, he said, from Exebridge on the border of Devon and Somerset. Reckoned he was a bit of both. Sort of mixed up, like.

I asked him whether, in his opinion, there was any particular difference between Devon and Somerset. Didn't think there was, he said, although on the whole he preferred Somerset. Why? I asked.

'Oh, I dunno,' he said. 'I reckon the women are easier.'

The impression you get is that the people of west Somerset are outspoken Celts. I asked a verger what his church was famous for, expecting to hear something about the bells or the rood screen.

'The vicar's wife,' said the man. 'She drinks fair *turrible*.'

SEVERN, POTTERIES AND PEAK

Once over that great estuary and into Wales by way of the Honddu Valley through Offa's Dyke, I felt that nothing could hold me back. I had beaten Dartmoor under the worst of conditions.

The principal attraction of the Honddu is the high-arched ruin of Llanthony Priory, which stands on a ledge, aloof, spectacular even in the rain. The guide tells you in lyrical Welshified English that it was 'the blessed St David who first made holy this ground'. The saint's name (Dewi) is perpetuated in scores of local shrines and wells.

A notice in the bar of the modern refectory (for tourists) says that originally two hermits, one of them a kinsman of William Rufus, lived there. The successors, a little band of monks, are said to have been very happy, for when they looked up, 'they beheld the tops of the mountains touching, as it were, the heavens and herds of wild deer feeding on the summits'. They prayed for divine support. To their consternation riches began to pour in. Two rich landowners, William and Hugh de Lacy, financed the building of the great priory. It was adopted by the Black Canons of the Order of St Augustine. Llanthony became an ecclesiastical centre and hundreds of people came to savour the solitude which their arrival destroyed.

But Providence, working in its inscrutable way, diverted most of the wealth to a daughter church in Gloucestershire, and until the dissolution of the monasteries the brotherhood lapsed into what one of their recorders describes as a laudable state of mediocrity.

In the oak-panelled gloom of the lodge next to the refectory I approached what I took to be a robed brother, only to find, when she turned round, that I was addressing a young handmaid of God.

'Is that where the Brothers meditated?' I asked, pointing to some outworks that might have been a cloister.

'No,' she said, smiling, 'that's where they washed their clothes.'

At eight o'clock you might have expected at least a glimmer of sunshine, but Darlaston, Barlaston, Trentham and Harford, all the towns that lead up to Stoke-on-Trent, were hidden in a gassy-smelling haze. Out of it loomed the gigantic, the strangely beautiful shapes of cooling towers. Behind them, like a ski-lift, chains of little buckets on wires trundle over mountains of coke. Here, you feel, is the basic architecture of industry; the power stations are verticals, marked by pencil-thin chimneys; the factories are flat blocks. There is nothing pretentious about the Potteries. They make things and what they can't sell they throw away. Behind the Doulton Works are mounds of shattered lavatory bowls, bedpans, bidets and basins. You can walk into Stoke by way of the Trent and Mersey Canal. The water that morning steamed and looked slightly

Chun Quoit

Wistman's dwarf wood

Wet going

iridescent. Two sad-looking swans, their under-plumage stained bright purple, cruised among bales of sodden hay and long streamers of toilet paper.

The banks of the canal are capped by large blocks of ferro-concrete. Some of them are remarkable for their wildly erotic engravings, executed, I suppose, before the concrete dried. On either side of the water the factories rumble and snort steam with predictable regularity. Squeezed in between them are allotments where contented-looking old men in shirt-sleeves grow sweet peas and Brussels sprouts and lean on their spades and gossip.

In the mid-morning bustle of Stoke I looked around for a laundry, a barber's shop and a place to get a good meal. The noise you remember here is the click of stiletto heels on broad flagstones, which sounds like a herd of startled deer.

In the help-yourself launderette a young girl took my little bundle of washing and pushed it into the whirler with her own. I noticed that from her large plastic bag she pulled out a man's shirt and man's underwear with a deft hand ungraced as yet by a ring.

The barber seemed puzzled by the lemon-yellow powder on his comb. 'Never seen dandruff like *that*,' he said. He was probably right. It was pollen from the sallows on the Shropshire Canal.

'Like another egg, love?' said the bulgy, bouncy, jolly-faced girl in the little cafeteria. She looked anxious. I still looked hungry and had already eaten four, as well as the bacon and tomatoes. There are no food problems in Stoke. I nodded. She looked pleased. I felt pleased. I like eggs. Come to think of it, I liked her too. Really bouncy, top and bottom. She slid another one on to my rind-littered plate.

'Out walking, mate?' enquired the man at the next table, conversationally. They are friendly people in Stoke. Old women are addressed as 'Mother', old men as 'Dad'. Male contemporaries are 'mate', and up to middle age the women say 'love'. After that you become 'Mister'. Men, as they remember them, are mostly on their allotments out of the way.

'Derbyshire,' I said. 'I'm heading for Dovedale.'

I told him how I proposed to follow the canal through Stoke until I got to the Churnet Valley.

'Could be difficult,' he said. 'Could be *quite* difficult.'

This, I discovered, was the understatement of the week. It wasn't just difficult. It was impossible. In at least four places the towpath was under water, the product of the rains of the previous month. This entailed elaborate detours through industrial slums.

THE PENNINE WAY

The best view of Edale, at the start of the longest signposted trail in England (240 miles), is from the crest of Hollins Cross, where an uncharitable notice on a gate says plainly that trespassers are liable to be shot. This is grouse-shooting country. Looking down, the impression is of a little Alpine valley seen through a glass darkly. To get the feel of the village you ought to meet the first train in on a Saturday morning, the 7.50 from Sheffield. Walkers spill out in droves.

By the time seven trains had arrived that morning Edale began to look like a country fair. It swarmed with hikers, bikers, nudists, naturalists, motorists, coach and train parties, day-trippers, weekenders, the purposive and the indolent.

The purposive promptly scuttled up the narrow track towards Kinder Scout like a pack of beagles. They wore enormous boots. They sang. They carried ropes and rucksacks. They were not seen again until nightfall. The indolents mooched about or wandered off quietly in search of a picnic place. Or somewhere to make love. And may God bless their union. A young clergyman confided that he walked in regularly from Glossop sustained only by orange juice and rye bread. Good for a rather delicate stomach, he said. He waved to a noisy coach party from a Stockport pub. Obviously pleased by clerical approval, they cheered and waved their beer bottles.

For those with a stake in the open-air business, Edale is a multiple store.

YORKSHIRE

Once you enter the West Riding of Yorkshire where I spent my youth, the dialect tends to be loud, declamatory and shorn of all superficialities.

Four locals in a transport café, including a bus conductor and a coalman, were discussing the obituaries in the *Hebden Bridge Times*, a staple topic of conversation on Fridays. Someone said Harry had gone out like a light. And wasn't that old neither, he wasn't. Hardly seventy-four. Looked full o' fettle, too. And he'd leave a packet, they reckoned. 'Bow-legged wi' brass, he was,' one of them added.

'And won't be wanting me this winter,' said the coalman thoughtfully.

Nobody laughed, but if you looked hard you could see an almost imperceptible relaxation of jaw muscles, which passes for amusement in the industrial riding. Death had been cauterised by a pungent platitude. The macabre humour stems from a long history of poverty when talk usually ranged round unemployment, the dole queue, sickness and

Offa's Dyke

The Potteries

*Dawn in
Staffordshire*

death. This survives still in an enormous repertoire of jokes calculated to horrify the stranger by the superficial denial of feeling.

'Where's t' wife?'

'Upstairs.'

'Takin' it easy?'

'Aye. She's dead.'

On this theme there are innumerable variations. One is of the neighbour who has come to pay his last respects. He stares long and earnestly at the deceased and says, 'Well, I must say she looks pretty good.' He pauses and then adds, 'Considering.' To this the husband says tartly, 'And she ruddy well should. She's just had a week at Blackpool.'

Close to the Border

High up in the north of England I trudged on, keeping to a stream that flowed away from the moor. 'Where am I heading for?' I asked an old man, expecting to be told the name of the next village. With what at that moment I took to be unseasonable humour, he said that if I kept going for sixty miles I would probably reach Newcastle-upon-Tyne. I thanked him and walked on to Carrigill, where I spent the night. It rained for seven hours. A local saying from which I derived no comfort is that if you can see Cross Fell it's going to rain, and if you can't it's raining.

To get into Scotland from Redesdale you can either cling to the forest road or cut up through the trees into the Cheviot Hills, holding to an ancient Roman highway called Dere Street that curls around Carter Bar and drops down into the valley of the Jed.

I went up into the hills at first light and got lost on what I took to be Ogre Hill, near the limit of the trees. The Cheviots are the highest and wildest part of Northumberland, a dome nearly twenty miles across. There are reputed to be the remains of Roman catapults up there. I couldn't find them, although the landscape has a distinctly Romanesque appearance. Straight tracks and rounded volcanic hills, grass-covered, with scarcely a rock to be seen. Below you could imagine, as perhaps the legionaries did, the plain of Latium. There is something Roman in the appearance of those Cheviot sheep with their aquiline noses and supercilious expressions. They are a very superior breed of sheep. I hurried on, climbing rapidly, conscious that most of the landmarks, even the distant peaks, were disappearing in the mist.

Here it was in the seventeenth century that little congregations of Presbyterians known as the Covenanters held holy service in secret.

The reformers had bound themselves by oaths to resist attempts made by Roman Catholics to regain their lost hold on Scotland. The Covenanters knew that they risked death if they were caught. The story is that during one of their congregations the famous preacher, the good man they called Savoury Mr Peden, was offering up thanks to God when, to his consternation, he saw a company of dragoons advancing up the hillside. Not wishing to alarm his flock, he concluded prayer with the words: 'And lastly, O Lord, cast the lap o' thy coat ower puir auld Sandy and his friends.' And they say that before the troopers reached them a mist rolled down from the heights of Broad Law and Mr Peden and his friends got safely away.

Border history is terrible stuff. One can understand the long fight for independence, the efforts to repel the constant incursions of the hated English. What the mind boggles at is the amount of treachery, feuding, cattle-lifting and slaughter that went on between Borderers at least nominally united against common enemies. On the English side the Charltons, Fenwicks, Herons and Melbournes were chronically at each other's throats, while on the other the Scotts raided the Kerrs, and the Grahams, Elliots, Turnbulls and Armstrongs joined in whenever it looked profitable. Throughout it all the law of retaliation prevailed. 'All is dishonorabell,' wrote Alexander Napier, 'quhair there is not eie for eie and tuith for a tuith.'

Scott o' Buccleuch slew Kerr's kinsfolk at Dornick; they in turn murdered auld Buccleuch in Edinburgh High Street. The aged Lady of Buccleuch, born a Kerr, was burned to death in her castle when her husband's men were out raiding with the English. Elliott of Stobs, a follower of Buccleuch at the time of the Dornick affair, ravaged the Scott country, killing scores of his fellow countrymen, including women and children. Lord Maxwell, dying on the field of battle, begged aid from Lady Johnstone, the wife of his adversary, who had come to the field to see how the day had fared. In a gesture of questionable charity, she dashed out his brains with the heavy keys of the castle. Fifteen years later Maxwell's son sought a 'friendly interview' with Sir James Johnstone with the avowed intent of patching up the quarrel. During a carefully arranged diversion he shot him in the back. The assassin fled to France, where he remained for four years. On his return he was betrayed by his kinsman, Sinclair, Earl of Caithness, and beheaded at Edinburgh.

Elements of the old strife linger on in the love of litigation. Only a Lowlander would confess to his minister that he knew of 'no greater pleasure on airth than a weel-gowin' law plea'. It lingers on too in the

Wappenshall

Industrial architecture

Norbury Junction

prickly regard for the honour of the family and the community, even where fighting is disguised under the name of football.

Late that night somebody in a pub in Jedburgh made a disparaging reference to one of the players in a forthcoming match. It brought the man next to me to his feet with a 'Wullie's a cousin o' mine and there's nobody here who'll gainsay *that!*' He banged his pot down and glared round aggressively. If yet another man called Erchie hadn't shaken his head slowly and decisively the incident might have ended in a brawl. Erchie neither upheld nor gainsaid the proposition. He merely acted as a reference point in a place where skill at arms is deeply respected.

Licensing laws in the Border country are notoriously lax. At about one o'clock in the morning when nearly everybody had sunk about seven pints of strong beer, a sad-faced youth stood up and began to sing the 'Ave Maria' for no reason I can recall. He sang it, moreover, in Latin, which seemed rather strange in a country dedicated to ridding the kirk of altar, candles and crucifix. The light tenor voice climbed up to the pinnacle of the *ad uxorem mundi*. It broke very slightly on the *exultimus* and rolled down on the *coelis advenit*. A splendid effort. Some of us began to think there were things in life more noble than bottled beer. Tears rolled unashamedly down my neighbour's cheeks.

'This kid can certainly sing,' I said to Erchie.

'Aye,' he said. 'He's had a lot of practice. He's just done three years in the Catholic reformatory at Gattonside.'

Kilt Lore

Borderers, as I understand it, may not wear Gaelic garb, and you next to never see it among native Highlanders, but expatriated Scots, especially those from overseas, delight in tartanry. In the bar of the Cross Keys in Peebles, a Mackay from Nova Scotia wore dark green, blue and black. He chatted to an Australian Campbell in a not dissimilar kilt, but with the addition of a yellow and white line. They explained the difference to me, carefully, while a red Hamilton from Ontario looked on. That night, at the great hydro outside the town, a building bigger than Buckingham Palace, the members of the Grocers' Federation were gloriously got up for their annual conference dinner. The Highland game is far from played out in the Lowlands.

TARTAN FRINGE

After walking since two o'clock in the morning I arrived at Callander in time for breakfast. I ate one in a café and another one at a hotel. Apart from the pubs and ice-cream parlours, the main street is almost entirely devoted to little shops that sell plaster models of Highland chieftains, Scottie dogs and tam-o'-shanters adorned with sprigs of plastic heather. Behind the trinket marts a handsome river flows out of Loch Venachar; there is also a parking lot the size of a football field. On the grassy green where I tried to sleep beside the river little girls came up and threw bread at me. They were, in fact, aiming inaccurately at some much overfed swans, which in Callander, I'm sure, touch nothing less than shortbread smeared with Dundee jam. The sight of the bread reminded me that I was still hungry. I took another snack and tried to settle down again, morbidly conscious that the town was filling up like a bath. Buses began to roll in, massive affairs from Glasgow and Dewsbury with built-in toilets and flags on the roof. The police shunted them into the parking lot and the population pressure built up on the green. Vendors shouted something that may have been Gaelic for Pepsi-cola or ice cream. It all sounded very strange. I was only half asleep when the City of Glasgow Police Pipe Band marched in with pipes skirling. I left them to it. There was a danger that the noise of pipes would set fire to the heather.

GLENS AND LOCHS

In trying to describe what it felt like to enter the Highlands that day I have the feeling of trying to recapture the beginning of a strange and lonely dream. From Cornwall to Callander I had grown used to my own company; I liked the feeling of being self-contained, but for most of the way I knew that villages were rarely far away. This is not so in the Highlands. I travelled not merely alone, but often without seeing a soul from one desolate glen to another.

Balquidder lies in a deep valley that runs approximately east–west. To get into the next parallel valley, Glen Dochart, I had the choice of going due north, direct, climbing over the crest of a steep escarpment, or keeping to the road that winds through Glen Ogle, a detour of several miles. In the church porch that morning I vowed that if I could find a direct track anywhere I had done with roads. The rain had ceased; the heights above were misty, but a notice-board at the foot of Kirton Glen pointed boldly to where I wanted to go and, rashly, I took a Forestry Commission sign at its face value.

The outcome is predictable. The old right of way had been turned into a horseshoe-shaped loggers' track that climbed up through the trees to a height of about 2,000 feet, turned round and, I suppose, came down again. At the apex of this disappointment I tried to get through something that resembled a path and eventually followed a steep burn through a firebreak until I found myself, alone and palely loitering, above the trees, but on the edge of an impressive *creag*. I cursed the commission, blackly, for this misdirection.

I sat up there for half an hour or so until the mist lifted; whereupon, on the very summit of the escarpment, I saw a little lochan, Eireannaich, steaming like a cup of tea. This gave me a map reference-point. I edged my way towards the water, worked round it and found a cleft through the *creag*. Far below, looking vast and uninviting on that grey morning, Glen Dochart extended as far as the eye could see. It began to rain again as I descended, but with visible landmarks I endured the soaking philosophically until I reached a disused railway in the valley, where I sought about for somewhere dry to spend the rest of the day.

Glen Dochart lies across Breadalbane – called Bridalbin – a tract of mountainous Perthshire that covers in all about 1,000 square miles. It gave noble title to the Campbells of Glenorchy and, in particular, to the first and infamous Sir John, author of the Glencoe Massacre, a man described as having neither honour nor religion but where they were mixed with interest. What you notice nowadays is that although the valleys seem fertile there is nobody about: the population has drifted away. Until I reached a hotel in Glencoe the following night I met very few people. 'What do you expect in Campbell country?' asked a West Highlander to whom I related my experience there.

Although it seemed months since I had trodden ancient railway tracks, the little bridges, the goblin-sized gradient signs and the rusty nails were oddly familiar. At the ghost station of Luib – *Luib* meaning the loop – you have the impression that the staff fled before the last train to Crianlarich pulled out. Clearly to be seen through cracked windows of a Lilliputian left-luggage office are dusty trunks, labelled suitcases, a bundle of fishing rods and a bicycle with flat tyres. What on earth happened that night when Stationmaster Campbell went home never to return? Nobody has yet been able to enlighten me.

A hard day's march up and over the infamous Pass of Glencoe lies Fort William. It still retains something of the atmosphere of a frontier post. The town itself has developed new industries, especially paper-making. It draws immense power from the water that thunders through a conduit buried under Ben Nevis, but, like so much of the west of Scotland, it

Jed Valley

82

depends essentially for its livelihood on visitors that come in by car and coach party.

I sought advice about how to work my way round Loch Arkaig and reach the coast opposite the Isle of Skye. A bearded young man in a kilt at the information centre warned me about a number of stages, especially Glen Dessary and those further on at Assynt in Sutherland. Dessary was an unexpected prevention. Assynt I knew about. In my imagination, it had already become the ultimate obstacle, but I had not anticipated trouble in a glen which I hoped to reach the following night.

As it looked as if I should be on my own for about eighty miles, I stocked up with several pounds of oatmeal, excellent stuff which can be mixed with water and eaten raw. This is what they call brose, but to make it a bit more palatable I bought some dried fruit, cheese and a few onions. With this compact if frugal fare I reckoned I could keep going for five days.

The Dead Vast

In the Highlands there is an old legend that at death the souls of fighting men are gathered up into the air, where for years they are cast backwards and forwards over the hills like migratory birds, unable to gain peace until they make expiation for their sins on earth. Sometimes on windy nights they can be heard fighting high up in the scudding clouds, and in the morning the rocks are spotted with blood. By putting on climbing gloves and shattering lumps of granite one against the other, I found many of those little rose-coloured stones in Glen Dessary. They are garnets.

Dessary is reckoned to be one of the most complicated geological formations in Britain. Earth movements over a period of many millions of years have folded the rocks back on themselves; those that were originally lying flat have been upended, bent into the shape of a horse-shoe and turned over so that now only the stumps of their feet are exposed. The walker is obliged to make elaborate detours, and five hours elapsed before I reached the narrow arm of the sea at Loch Nevis. Should you venture into that dead vast I warn you, solemnly, to watch out for the deceptively simple outlines of a mountain called Sroine. It lies four-square across the glen and beckons seductively towards Loch Morar, an easy primrose path into a cul-de-sac.

LOCAL FAUNA

At Finiskaig on Loch Nevil the shallow water is tufted with salty sam-
phires and glassworts, and there an eagle rose, startled at my approach,
clutching something alive and dangling from extended talons. A rabbit,
it seemed, or maybe a young hare. With easy wing-beats it gained
height rapidly, making for a cliff face. At this two ravens pitched off a
pinnacle and attacked it in mid-air. One robber kept to short-range
tactics, pecking, fluttering, seeking to distract the laden bird, while the
other repeatedly swooped down from on high. The grunts and barks
sounded dog-like. The result, I thought, was a foregone conclusion.
Surely the hard-pressed bird would drop its prey. But with occasional
side-slipping movements and an almost leisurely swerve of its great
wings, the eagle seemed strangely unconcerned. All three birds passed
out of sight behind the cliff, where for several minutes I could still hear
the clamour. Eagles, they say, can lift ten pounds in weight: one was
seen to carry a struggling wild cat to a height of 1,500 feet before
dropping it to its death on the rocks below.

This is red deer country. Groups of hinds with scampers of fawns at
foot grazed unconcernedly in meander pastures where, thanks to the
downwind and the thunder of the stream, I often saw them before they
scented me. Usually the alarm came not from the herd, but from an old
matriarch, isolated on sentinel duty high over the river. The short,
explosive bark was repeated first by one hind and then another until a
dozen animals with forelegs partly raised for a quick getaway swung
round in my direction. And then off they ran with youngsters protec-
tively encircled. Bits of shale tinkled down the slope long after they had
gone.

Although the sexes congregate only for about six weeks in each year,
red deer are intensely social animals. The stags have a club life of their
own. On high crests at sundown I got a glimpse of heavily antlered
animals in dramatic postures. But never near at hand. I often wondered
where they went during the day.

I had reason that night to wonder where I was going myself, for I
missed the track to Barrisdale and felt tired. Instead of trying to climb
out of the glen, I swung east and followed a tributary of the Carnach
to the head of Loch Quoich. There I settled down to a nourishing if
uninspiring meal of oatmeal and raisins. I lit a fire for company, but
put it out before I went to sleep.

Throughout the night came the sound of gentle squeaks and blab-
bering noises. The deer were talking to each other. I had pitched down
where the tent would be least conspicuous and this proved rewarding
at dawn when, by peering through a gap in the fastening, I had an
intimate view of their family life.

Half a dozen fawns scampered about like lambs, chasing each other, butting and frolicking, racing up and down hillocks, often falling flat on their noses. The games were broken off, temporarily, when they returned to the hinds for yet another suck. And then off they went again. Like lambs, too, they were disposed to bounce into the air as if on springs. Or else they sniffed at the dewy sedge grass or rolled over, kicking legs that seemed too spindly to support them.

In between gambolling and feeding they are licked vigorously by the hinds, usually about the eyes and ears, an action which appears to give both parties intense pleasure, the calves particularly, since they almost invariably lift up their muzzles for more.

From Ardelve, the centre of a clover-leaf of lochs – Alsh, Duich and Long – on the mainland but within sight of the Isle of Skye, I slouched north east to Nonach on the advice a village constable who said his very, very old friend there, the keeper of the big estate, would put me right in no time at all. The keeper wasn't at home, but his dogs were, and what seemed at first to be a particularly friendly black and white

Loch Arkaig

sheepdog, one of several, ensured remembrance by battening on to my right calf. I beat him off with a small Japanese camera and ran off until I remembered I ought to be limping. Exuberant bleeding, but no evidence of torn muscle. I plastered myself up and followed the River Ling for miles and miles until I got lost in a *dubh*, or black water – that is, a stream which winds through peat hags. That night I hoped to be in the little hamlet of Achnashellach, no great distance ahead, but detached from me by a range to the west that could only be scaled by mounting an impressive corrie. And there things went distinctly wrong.

June 11: Seems I'm stuck on this damned ledge for the night Followed R. Ling into tree-lined gulley. Discovered too late that map and field glasses had fallen from ripped jacket pocket. Went back. Unable to find them. Abandoned stream for 1,000 ft contour and descended to eerie-looking Loch Laoigh. Mounted corrie, remembering what I could of the track bearing. Reached crest to discover northern face drops sheer. Looks

Glencoe

87

foul. Sought about for path down to the east. Found new-born deer shivering in hollow. Fur wet. Seems unable to stand. Cloud blew across like smoke. Visibility about 10 ft. Am staying until it lifts. . . .

Towards dusk the rim of the cloud layer below came rose-pink. Out of that highly chromatic cotton wool a bird – a hawk of some kind – appeared for an instant. It circled once or twice, then sank back again, like the fin of a fish seen through the ice of a pond. Soon afterwards, I edged into the layer myself, to find it even danker and darker than I feared. A step off the track brought me to the edge of something that fell away into the gloom. Imagining precipices on all sides, I put up my tent and settled down in more comfort than I deserved.

June 12: Awoke to find that I had slept on a track about a mile from Achnashellach Railway Station. Am undaunted by lack of valour, since ridge behind looks far steeper than it did from the top. Bitten calf looks a bit puffy, but apparently not symptom of sepsis, as other calf looks even puffier. Waded across river to Youth Hostel for breakfast, where agreeable young man in charge accompanied me to Beinn Eighe Nature Reserve, about twelve miles away. Treated myself to half-day holiday to brace up for what looks like arduous eagle-watching exercise tomorrow, with a knowledgeable warden called Dick Balharry.

June 13: Left Balharry in Dundonnell. Struck out for place on south-western shore of Loch Broom where he thought I ought to be able to pick up ferry for Ullapool. Arrived at dusk. The cliff-tops, the last reputed breeding place of the sea eagle, looked like the edge of the world. Immense vista, crinkly sea, toothy-looking rocks and islands in a Wagnerian sunset. Lights of what I took to be the very best Ullapool restaurants just visible on the opposite shore, but they might as well be a thousand miles away as there's no bloody ferry. Local Charon seems to have gone on strike together with his chums, who forced me to make frustrating detours to the south. May their bowels burst! Place deserted. Bathed feet. Two more toenails missing. But still got six. Mooched about looking for somewhere to sleep. Came across partly constructed dream house of man who was building it for his ailing wife. Hospitably received by them both and crossed the loch next morning in boat carrying their workmen.

Ullapool is a bright little port that has gone over to tourism, lock, stock and what used to be the fish barrel. Nowadays the boats take visitors round the islands. Everyone seems to be doing fine. You can't see the quay for the cars, and there are queues for the boats and almost everything else.

OUTERMOST GAELDOM

In a deck chair on the beach the question was whether to get it over
and done with by belting along to where the climb began. Or play it
cool and hole up somewhere. At this point I went to sleep, for I felt
extraordinarily tired.

I slept for three hours and then made for Inchnadamph. The route is
across country, to Strathkannaird and then up the road north into
Sutherland. You can't avoid the so-called highway, for it takes advan-
tage of all the available gaps in the range. It cuts through the death-grey
Cambrian limestone, Moine schists and compressed sand as old as any
in Europe. Here, bunched together, is the whole geological history of
Scotland.

'Got to get to Cape Wrath tonight,' said the man with the boiling
radiator. I didn't ask why, because he might have asked me the same
question.

On the River Kannaird I got into a strange argument about the sexu-
ality of mayflies with three unusually masculine-looking women in
waders who had been fishing in a pool above Blughasary. 'Is this a
female?' one of them asked, producing a specimen with three tails. And
all I could say was it looked that way, although the sexes were sometimes a bit confused.

At Elphin, a village only in name, the occupants of a few cars and
caravans were whooping it up around the noisy light of a primus stove.
They sang the 'Couper o' Fife' and the 'Ball of Kirriemuir', but without
much enthusiasm. Two American girls detached themselves with some
difficulty from some amorous youths on motorcycles. They were anxious
that I should not think they were really complaining about the simple
ardour of the Gaels. 'Nothing *wrong* with them,' as one of them put it,
'but I guess your town boys are steadier.'

Late that night I was within five miles of Inchnadamph and looked for
somewhere to sleep. A hillock beside a stream seemed pleasant enough,
but the sight of a man putting up a tent drew first one caravan and
then two more off the road. I had started yet another little colony.
    Unfortunately I had chosen a very bad site. It hummed, not only
with mosquitos, but with black flies, little needle-point-sized creatures
said to be responsible for the Highland fling. Hoping that the cara-
vanners wouldn't think it downright unsociability on my part, I packed
up and went higher up the braeside. They watched me go. I turned
round and waved my hands, violently, trying to give the impression

89

that I was swatting at flies, but at that distance it probably looked like *Beyond Dessary*
an abusive gesture.

Behind the hotel at Inchnadamph you climb up a sheep track for about
two miles, mounting steadily, keeping to the contours of Droighinn to
avoid the twists and turns of the stream in the gorge below. I sweated
profusely. It felt sultry. The storm still hung above, and though it was
mistier there than I had anticipated, I assumed hopefully that peaks
hidden behind a distant bluff were still visible. At about 1,200 feet it
brightened up and so did I. The top of the corrie appeared just where
I had been told it would, and I looked out for the little lochan, Cuaran,
on top of the ridge. To celebrate at what seemed at least Camp One, I
sat down and had a drink, a remarkably untimely celebration as it
turned out.

Eilean Donnan

The track let me down disgracefully – or rather I disgraced myself by hurrying along, almost trotting at a time when I should have trodden more carefully on the loose stones. In fact I was staring ahead at that most nebulous of opponents, a wall of mist or cloud. I could see it rolling down – not fast, but implacably, blotting out everything it touched. I reckoned, wrongly, that if I hurried I could get round the neck of the corrie and on to firmer ground before it enveloped me.

Something gave way underfoot. I lost my balance and slid down about thirty feet of scree. No damage. I was scarcely scratched. The rucksack acted as a toboggan, but there I was on the banks of a stream that fell over the edge of a cliff. Frightened? I was shit-scared, as we said in the army. But what do you do? Bawl for help? There wasn't a soul for miles. I don't know what the professional does on such an occasion. What I did was to collect and try to identify all the little plants within an arm's reach, merely for something to do.

The mist still hung about. I can't go on like this for long, I thought. But I did. For perhaps two hours. And then some thrice-blessed visibility. Enough at least to see for about fifty yards. I couldn't move more than a few feet without starting a little avalanche of gravel, but there seemed no alternative but to go on, again, upwards, laboriously.

Curious lighting effects caused the enveloping mist to flicker like a faulty fluorescent tube. This happened two or three times. I stopped, expecting a fearful crash of thunder. Instead, more flickers. The crags stood out momentarily. And then from far, far away came a noise more like a groan than thunder.

The sole of one of my shoes became detached at the toe and I tried to sew it up with waxed thread, using a flat stone to push the needle into the sodden leather. The marvel is they had lasted so long. I scrambled on, uncomfortably, keeping to a strict compass course, swinging off only when the ground dipped or rose more steeply than I felt competent to tackle in the gloom. I reached what I took to be the little loch, followed the western shore for about a quarter of a mile and then continued north east until it looked as if I had got over the ridge.

A steep ridge. Not a *creag*, I hoped fervently. Rock everywhere. No vegetation. No sound. Still gloomy, but it looked brighter ahead. Down below I saw the dim outlines of not one but innumerable lochs, irregular in shape, merging one with another. Nothing big enough to be Loch Shin as I imagined it, but they all seemed to be in the right direction.

Down I went into a deep gulley, a rift that swung first north east, then north. Not the most encouraging direction, certainly, but there was no way out. I could go back or I could go on. There was no track of any sort to follow on those sloping plates of grey-black gneiss. On I went, still down into bleak uncertainty. The gully led into a narrow valley with towering cliffs on both sides.

By that time both shoes were in pretty poor shape. The sole of one flapped about and the stitching of the other had come loose in several places. To make things worse, a strap of the rucksack had broken in the fall. I had the feeling that the expedition was dropping to bits.

What I needed for encouragement more than anything else was a glimpse of Loch Shin, the end of the difficult pathfinding part of the trip. But where was it? Twice I saw what might have been water far ahead, but it might equally have been quartzite or a shaft of light on wet rock.

About six o'clock that night a loch loomed far down in the gorge-like valley and I descended towards it, slowly. I felt excessively tired. The water was far from where I expected to see it, but I imagined, hopefully, that I had swung round towards the eastern end of Shin. Hope changed to apprehension when the water appeared to curl away in the wrong direction, to the west.

I scrambled down to within two hundred yards of the shore. A flock of seabirds flapped off. I looked down at them in utter dejection. Instead of Loch Shin I had dropped down to the sea loch Glencoul, on the coast. There was no way out, for the cliffs were precipitous, and I had no alternative but to go back.

A bad evening. The grey shawl of mist still hung round the top of the gorge. The rocks I had hopefully scrambled down earlier seemed twice as steep on the way back. I recall only a few landmarks: one, a prostrate pine, its bone-white roots sticking up in the air like a petrified octopus; another, an enormous waterfall, the famous Chual Aluinn, the biggest uninterrupted drop in Britain. It fell down with the noise of escaping steam. It seemed to cascade out of the sky, for the crest was hidden in the mist.

How I had managed to stray down to Glencoul became compass-clear far too late for comfort. The sweep of the gorge had beguiled me away from harder going, over the wall of the valley. From there it took me another three hours to get down to Loch Shin.

Once down from those heights there are no *creags* or chasms. Only manure-coloured water and olive-grey bog gently rising and falling for miles and miles. I squelched along. Two of my six remaining toenails fell off. Not painfully. New pink ones appeared, miraculously, underneath.

The red ribbon of the northern light lay low along the west. Scarcely any mist, but almost dark now, the silence heavy and the sense of loneliness profound. No jubilation when the much sought loch appeared, for in the dark I could scarcely see.

There at Corriekin, within a mile of the long-looked-for loch, after I had been walking for fifty days, the most difficult part of the trip came to an end at midnight in the lodge of a good shepherd and his wife. The man had driven off down the valley to look at a prizefight on a neighbour's television set and his wife had waited up for him. They treated me with heart-touching hospitality.

END OF THE AFFAIR

Clouds over Achnashellach

Finishing line: Duncansby Head

Altnaharra Hotel is filled with rich sportsmen. That morning early, some tinkers on bicycles who said cautiously that they came from Dundee were netting the outfall of the Naver with what looked like lace curtains. Later in the day, at intervals on the banks of the river, were parked large chauffeur-driven cars whose English owners, with a gillie at hand, cast flies into the coffee-coloured water. Nobody I saw caught anything. And on I walked to the windy sea at Bettyhill.

The village lies some thirty miles to the east of Cape Wrath, a corruption, they tell you locally, of *Hvarf*, the turning point, the place where the captains of the Norse ships pushed their helms hard over and turned sail down the west coast of Scotland.

On that coast I turned east towards John o' Groats. This is another corner of Norse Britain. Here it was that Earl Thorfinn the Mighty governed the Orkneys, the Shetlands, the Western Isles and nine provinces of Gaeldom. The place names tell the story. There is Spyta, Skakker, Skirsa, Mireland, Brawl and Barrack. In Thorfinn's time there was gold in the rivers and pearls for barter.

> 17 June: left Bettyhill at sunrise and scurried along the coast road with only fifty miles to go. Scenery bleak and windswept: undulating moors with worn-down outcrops of tortured rock. Granite churches with raised pine-wood pulpits in place of altars. At Melvick crossed into even flatter, windier Caithness, which apparently means wild cat country. Two pubs filled with local seamen getting drunk on strike pay, but less aggressively by far than in the Lowlands. Spent night in dismal lodgings in Dounreay where duralumin sphere of atomic station reactors looks like a golf ball to be driven off into North Atlantic.

Only thirty miles to go now. I strode on, faster. Past Lybster with an enormous view of a crinkly sea, the home, one might think, of that fabled monster, the Kraken. On I went. Past Thuster and Scrabster where, instead of hedges and walls, the rock-littered pastures are divided up by what look like long lines of gravestones. They are, in fact, Caithness flags, thin slabs of Devonian sandstone. Looking at them, I thought of faraway Devon and Cornwall. Similar moors, similar cliffs: John o' Groats resembles Land's End. On each headland a gaunt hotel and in front of each hotel a photographer with coat collar turned up and hands in his pockets. He stands next to a clever bit of salesmanship, a portable signpost with adjustable directions.

'Where are you from?' he asks. Manchester, Minneapolis? No matter where. He has a box of all the letters of the alphabet and you can be photographed against an arm of the post that points to your home town, together with the mileage. Price ten shillings and sixpence, post free. The cliff-top concessions in Cornwall and Caithness are run by the same enterprising man.

Only twenty miles to go now. Down to the harbour quarter of new-built Thurso, a bright, attractive, angular place, like a bit of modern jewellery. And then on to Dunnet and Kirk o' Tang.

'Walked far?' asked the motorist, pulling up.

'Pretty far,' I said, with carefully contrived nonchalance. But when he asked how far and I told him, he drove off looking, I think, more saddened than surprised. Thank God he didn't ask why.

Far out to sea rose Stroma. And then Hoy and Ronaldsay and the other isles of Orkney. Here is the very end of Britain. The wind blew hard. It blew me sideways, but with the end in sight, a distant point of land narrowing mile by mile, I could have withstood a hurricane. Only ten miles to go.

Ten miles to what? To a mere name on a map? What had it all amounted to? Why hadn't I spent more time seeing fewer places more leisurely, using a car here and there? I finished the journey as I had started two months earlier, by asking myself a lot of questions. The difference was I could now answer some of those I had thought most about.

The walk came to an end at a craggy-looking place called Duncansby Head, a mile or two beyond John o' Groats. There, from the cliff-tops, I looked down on the outermost tip of Gaeldom, a flurry of water and black rock. I turned round and walked back to the hotel in the greenish twilight. I ate supper, alone, wrote up a few notes and sat down on the edge of a small bed, flicking back through the pages of a diary filled with vigorous facts and names that already seemed rather strange and faraway.

Journey to the Jade Sea

How It All Began

AFTER EXCURSIONS into the fringe of the Arctic and the Congo I began to get itchy feet again, a feeling fortified by my jaunt through Britain, and I knew where I wanted to go. Back to Africa.

At Arusha in Tanzania, at the end of yet another international congress known to us, the science writers, as the 'Woof Woofs' (World Wildlife Fund), some senior game wardens, anxious to demonstrate their own conservation problems, offered to drive me back to northern Kenya in stages.

At Wamba in the NFD – the Northern Frontier District of Kenya – I developed acute backache and became so frustrated looking at the spectacular scenery through the dusty windscreens of Land-rovers that I suggested that we might indulge in a *safari kidogo*, a little excursion. Thanks largely to Gaston de Witte in the Congo, I wasn't too bad at what is still known among African Whites as *Ki-settler*, a very rudimentary form of Ki-swahili.

A sympathetic fellow who'd been out there since he left the King's African Rifles with decorations shepherded me up a mountain of ancient rock called Lolokwi. At the top he waved his arms airily towards what he called euphemistically 'the square root of Fanny Adams'. I looked to the north east and north west, toward deserts with an apocalyptic quality – utterly stark and relieved only by the stumps of worn-out volcanoes. What life there may have been there had long since been burnt out by the sun.

Without giving much thought to ways and means I told him that if he could name a worthwhile objective I would return to Wamba as soon as I could and cross the desert on foot. To my surprise he didn't seem particularly taken aback and said he thought Lake Rudolf would be a good place to head for. That night he told me a lot about the green lake among the lava fields, the lake which I called the Jade Sea. From

Scene from Lolokwi

99

what he said of its varying moods, sometimes tempestuous, sometimes womb-like in its oceanic peace, it seemed wholly appropriate that Rudolf should have been named after the neurotic Crown Prince of Austria who committed suicide at Mayerling after shooting his mistress through the head.

This, then, is the story of a fortunate journey towards the strip of water that lies across the border of Kenya and Ethiopia; I say fortunate because to reach Lake Rudolf and return via the Turkana shore we covered about 1,100 miles on foot, and we covered them without serious mishap, at least to ourselves, if not to the camels. I had almost no qualifications for making a foot safari, certainly nothing in the way of previous experience. It was the first time I had been into the bush without another European on hand. I knew nothing about guns and gear and as for the camels, those gangling, good-natured beasts, I had seen them previously only through the bars of a zoo.

In Nairobi and elsewhere the big agencies sell safaris, expensively, but as simply available as oysters on the open shell. Bush experience can be bought complete with kit, transport and guides at a cost of between £2,000 and £3,000 per month. I had to watch my pocket. I borrowed six camels, hired others and bought a few for less than five pounds each. The men received sixty Kenyan shillings a month and when I eventually got the feel of a distinctly unfamiliar rifle I shot most of what we ate. Looking back on the trip I regret little except my initial incompetence.

I am tempted to say that bush experience can be picked up pretty quickly but, remembering the stupid things I did during the first week or two, I would advise anyone as inexperienced as I was to watch local *expertise* and try to improve on it. Some things, of course, can't be picked up quickly. There is no short cut to the language problem or the difficulty of getting used to the sun. I tackled both problems together by baking myself on the deck of a Nile stern-wheeler and arguing in elementary Ki-swahili with anyone who came up to tell me that I was mad. The result was that before I reached Wamba I could put simple questions to Africans who couldn't speak English and, equally impor-tant, I could walk about with nothing on except sneakers, a pair of shorts and a bush hat decked out with an ostrich feather which, I discovered, helped to keep the flies off.

Gear, especially important things like rope and sacks for the camel loads, can be bought in one sitting at any one of half a dozen stores in Nairobi, but a word of warning here. The man in charge of the expedition needs good advice before he starts, and I had the very best available from that prince of modern travellers, Wilfred Thesiger. He advised me, among other matters, to take a lot of medicine instead of useless trinkets and knick-knacks, and to wear and carry cheap dispensable sneakers instead of expensive, sweaty bush boots.

To reach Wamba I flew to Khartoum and sailed up the Nile as far as Juba in the Sudan. After a period of acclimatisation among the white rhinos of West Nile, another game warden ferried me down the length of Lake Albert on the Uganda/Congo border and passed me on to a colleague who was on safari in Semliki. I spent a couple of weeks in Karamoja in eastern Uganda, where the Turkana people were at odds with the Dodoth. Thereafterwards I thought only of what I should do when I hooked a lift to Wamba, a habitation of about fifteen dilapidated huts a little over 100 miles south of Lake Rudolf. There I hoped to pick up a string of camels. They told me that everything would be in order when I got there.

THE SHAKE-DOWN

At Wamba almost everything went wrong. The local game warden had gone home on leave. Eight camels hired on my behalf had been left in the care of an idle fellow who had allowed them to champ away at the wrong sort of browse. By the time I arrived all of them were very, very sick and one had died. They said it was mange. Another warden, a very distinguished man, came in from an adjacent station and tried to hire some beasts from the local Veterinary Department, but he doubted whether even healthy animals could carry as much gear as I had brought from Nairobi. Resolving to jettison about forty tins of corned beef, two dictionaries and some historical works on the discovery of the Northern Frontier District, I faced other problems.

The most pressing was the question of an escort. Because the Marille tribesmen from Ethiopia were said to be on the rampage with guns, the District Commissioner insisted that if I wanted to travel beyond a point less than one third of the way up the eastern shore of the lake, I must be accompanied by armed men and 'somebody reliable'. I referred this unexpected setback to my resourceful friend the game warden, who said, good fellow that he was, that he thought he could bring in a squad of *askaris* from Marsabit, a mountain post out to the north east, in Rendille country. I turned to my staff.

Everyone wanted to say something. A man introduced as my syce or camel leader seemed distinctly surly. A red-painted fellow, with bones like napkin rings in his dangling ears, he tried to explain through a giggling interpreter that he had wife trouble and was unanxious to leave a girl worth at least sixty cows to the attentions of a rival brave. I had to say something. I had been told that the Swahili for 'yes' (*n'dio*), 'good' (*m'zuri*) or 'maybe' (*labda*) were effective substitutes for almost any positive statement of opinion. Diffidently I tried *m'zuri*. To my dismay the man also said 'good' and went back to his red-painted paramour.

If I understood them aright, other men on my pay-roll were complaining that they had been told that the safari would last at least three months. They had hoped, they said, to be back in Wamba in about three weeks' time. Ignoring the interpreter and muttering what I hoped was Swahili for 'Yes, three months, definitely,' I passed on. They looked horrified.

A third fellow, a man with an atrocious tic like a wink, was anxious to sell what appeared to be the middle portion of a fair-sized snake wrapped up in coconut matting. '*Kamba?*' he kept asking. '*Kamba?*' Not knowing what *kamba* was and suppressing a ridiculous desire to wink back, I turned it down.

Besides diarrhoea, I had an acute attack of nervous indigestion and an ominous feeling that brave words spoken far away about undertaking a long trip essentially on my own were no more than that – brave, idle words.

Perhaps all safaris start this way. Somewhat despondently I sat down among the food and gear piled up on the game warden's verandah. Trying to ignore the snake-seller who crouched down at the foot of the steps looking up at me like a faithful dog, I opened the only package which seemed important at that moment. It contained half a dozen bottles of Scotch.

Wilfred Thesiger, who is something of a stoic, had advised me to avoid fancy tinned stuff and buy as much rice as I could carry. I bought sixty pounds. Memories of school dinners. It seemed a mighty amount of rice. I had also started out from Nairobi with about forty pounds of sugar; from the crunch on the floor it was apparent that the abrasive processes of a foot safari had already begun. I traced the leak back to a hole caused by the protrusive leg of a badly packed Primus stove.

Thesiger had also warned me that camels were intolerant of tins and boxes, but they could carry almost anything stowed away in floppy sacks or kit-bags. Bags formed well and they could be lashed around the animals' flanks or laid across their backs.

I had bought thirty empty sacks, twelve kit-bags and forty calico bags about a foot square. By putting the food in labelled bags and the bags in labelled sacks, I managed to reduce the whole load to about 1,400 pounds. This included half a hundredweight of dried camel meat (emergency supplies) and 200 pounds of maize meal (*posho*) for the men. It was doubtful whether a string of mangy camels could stand up under this load, but I couldn't think of anything else I could leave behind. However, I had forgotten that we needed at least sixteen gallons of water, a large box of ammunition and about £150 in cash, mostly in small notes and East African shillings.

Somebody came up behind me. I shut the cash box guiltily and turned to find a bullet-headed man who wore only a faded rose-coloured blanket, patched like the sail of a barge. '*Effendi*,' he began, opening his hands in an expressive gesture of welcome and respect.

I recognised the man, vaguely, although I couldn't remember his name and was somewhat disconcerted by being addressed as *effendi*. I had no desire to wrestle with Arabic as well as Swahili.

But Karo, the son of Lapali, was not a Muslim. A wandering Samburu, he had been in many places, including gaol. He proved to be a man of infinite resource and not a little cunning. When we had trouble in the camp, Karo was usually at the bottom of it; yet when I had trouble from outside it was to Karo that I turned. Nevertheless, his presence on that hot and harassing afternoon in Wamba proved something of an embarrassment.

I went through a series of conversational openings which I had carefully rehearsed in advance. First a hearty *jambo* to which he replied no less cordially. How were his affairs? His affairs, he said, were well. Was he from Wamba? No? Then where was his *manyatta*, his homestead? He said it was near Mount Kulal, far away to the north where the Samburu merged with the Rendille. Eventually I asked him what he wanted.

The question tended to wreck the rest of the conversation because Karo answered in a torrent of Swahili. I nodded without knowing what it was all about. When he shook his head and shrugged his shoulders I did the same. In fact, if he hadn't pushed his right hand forward as if to grasp a crisp twenty-shilling note, I might have made the mistake of saying 'good' for the second time in one afternoon, thereby parting with yet another pound to an incorrigible cadger.

I shook my head slowly, sorrowfully. Karo also looked a little sad; then his face lit up with a huge grin. 'Good,' he said. 'Good!' Thinking that I had got around one minor staff problem, I felt pretty good too. Karo stayed for about half an hour and looked at everything laid out on the verandah floor. He fingered the sacks, squeezed the bags and peered into everything that could be opened or unfastened. I was surprised that he could even identify the dried camel meat and the *pangas* wrapped up in straw, but he probed about and pronounced everything 'good' or 'very good' or 'not *very* good'. This condemnation was mild enough and rare, but it seemed so absolute in its implication that I was tempted to throw the inadequate articles away. They included most of my rope.

As I had bought about 300 yards in Nairobi, this was a distinct disappointment. Some of the sisal was rough to the touch; I felt somewhat diffident about it, but Karo seemed more concerned about the soft cotton stuff, the very best I could buy. After watching him hold a length between his teeth and nod his head approvingly, I gathered that it would make good head ropes or halters for the camels. But I could not understand why he frowned when he threw a loop round his bare waist and pulled it from side to side, like a tailor with a tape measure. 'Not very good,' he said.

'Why not good?'

Karo got down on his hands and knees: obviously he had become a camel. He groaned as a camel would groan as it lifted a load and then, as he rose on to his toes and finger-tips, he allowed the rope to slip round his waist until he was holding it with one hand in the small of his back. Without knowing much Swahili I understood that cotton rope was liable to slip and was not good enough for a camel girth. Yet the problem remained. I had no other rope. I shrugged my shoulders. Too bad. What was I expected to do?

Karo continued to speak rapidly. I caught only one vaguely familiar word out of the babble of explanation. It was *kamba*. But what was *kamba*?

Mezek at work

Karo with Mezek

Outside in the dusk the snake-seller with the atrocious tic moved a step nearer, expectantly, and Karo motioned him on to the verandah. What had appeared to be snake wrapped in coconut matting was a tight, cylindrical coil of pliant bark rope, plaited by the vendor's wife. They were camel girths. They cost five shillings each and I bought seven lengths, one for each camel. They were about the most useful things I bought in Wamba and their utility was undiminished even when I learnt some time afterwards that the vendor's wife was Karo's sister. The wandering Samburu would go to extraordinary lengths, even to do someone a good turn.

Late that night I sat in the game warden's house, half listening to a professional argument between my host and a white hunter who had looked in on his way up country. It had something to do with the local close seasons for hunting. My mind was on other matters. I was due to leave at eight o'clock the next morning. There was still some doubt about replacing my head camel leader, although several men were said to have applied for the job. Everything seemed to turn on the following day.

I asked about the men who had objected to a safari likely to last longer than three months. Apparently I had made another mistake. The warden explained that the question put to me that morning was whether the safari would last more than three weeks (*weeki*): the men were anxious to get long-term employment. It seemed that I had shaken my head and by confusing the word for month or moon (*m'wozi*) with *m'waka* (meaning year) I had said, 'Yes, definitely three years.' Their dismay was understandable.

Would things be different in the morning? Were the camels really sick? Question after question spun round in my head like waltzing mice. So much depended on the next day. Tomorrow and tomorrow. . . .

To my surprise the day dawned like any other. Doves droned from the top of the acacias; a metallic-green starling looked at me sideways through a bright yellow eye and walked off, chuckling. At half-past six only the birds and I and a lethargic houseboy were up and about. I fidgeted and looked at my watch; he laid out breakfast with the alacrity of a two-toed sloth.

At seven o'clock I tried to put breakfast forward by half an hour without disclosing how nervous I felt, how urgently I wanted to be out and away, anywhere. The feeling of complete dependence on the opinion of authority was an embarrassment. The warden clearly knew too much; the hunter was laconic. For these people safari had become an orderly business as stylised as packing a weekend suitcase, looking up a train and ordering a taxi to the station. They *enjoyed* their breakfast; they

ordered more coffee and chatted about totally unimportant things like home leave and the exorbitant cost of fishing tackle. I fed my dyspepsia on unchewed toast and made it worse.

Ready for loading

By eight o'clock there was still no sign of the local tribesmen who had been hired to get me over the mountains and into the desert. They had probably deserted and, like as not, taken most of my gear with them. Nonsense, the warden said. What I needed was another cup of coffee. The camels had to be rounded up and driven in from some browsing grounds at the back of the warden's house. It might take hours. Breathing an over-breathy whistle, as if the whole affair was completely under control, I sauntered over to an immense pile of boxes and fiddled about with my unused guns.

At a quarter past eight came a sudden babble of voices and bellowing of beasts from the compound in front of the house. The warden rose to look out of the window. 'Your camels,' he said, 'have arrived.'

Apprehension promptly turned to a mild feeling of panic. Up to that point I had been a traveller only by dubious virtue of preparation. Innumerable problems had arisen, but I had been comforted by the thought that at any moment and at relatively small cost I could call the whole expedition off. Now I appeared to be in charge of a circus of dilapidated animals and men. I had hired it at long range and at the very least I was obliged to see it through the first act. The camels were being driven down a little hill at the back of the house by an excited mob of villagers. They may have been sick animals, but my first impression was of a troupe of comedians. They lurched about as if drunk.

They wheeled in front of the house and at the command '*Toa! Toa!*' they flopped down, apparently already exhausted by a journey of a quarter of a mile. A tough little man in a peaked cap and the uniform of a game scout shouted something incomprehensible and then marched stiffly towards me. This was my headman, Lelean. He gave me a crashing butt salute and said we were ready to load.

Looking back I think now that we must have established an all-time record. The details are a little vague because I took almost no part in the proceedings and was surprised by everything I saw. Somebody produced a bundle of mats; somebody else untied a bundle of sticks about eight feet in length and no thicker than a bean-pole. The mats or *herios* were thrown over the backs of the camels, two in front and two behind. The sticks were matched, divided into groups of four and, by the deft manipulation of the back rope woven by Karo's sister, a double V of framework was built up on each flank. These were the wooden supports, the *miti* to which the loads were lashed.

I wandered among the loading parties, trying to give the impression of an old safari hand prepared to be a bit indulgent on the first day.

When most of the shouting was over and the villagers stood back from the trussed beasts, Lelean marched over and gave me another crashing salute.

'It is prepared,' he said. This time I ventured a carefully phrased 'Good! Let us go.' Farewells were exchanged. The camels were kicked in the rear. They rose to their feet, noisily, and then babbling, bubbling and breaking wind, they staggered forward on the long journey towards the Jade Sea.

First Day Out

Within ten minutes we were out of sight of the village and making for a gap in the mountains as clear cut as the rear sight of a rifle. The going was easy, the scenery superb and the sky pale blue with no more than a wisp of genial cloud. Looking back on the disordered events of departure, I can remember nothing more clearly than the enormous sense of relief that the preliminaries were over and done with. Now I was on my own; I felt as if I had run away from school. Even the camels looked less grotesque than before.

Away to the right the face of the Matthews rose like a wall and disappeared into the distance which extended for about forty miles and then merged into the N'doto Hills. I should have liked to continue north and thereby avoid crossing the mountains, but somewhere on the far side of the Matthews lay the forestry station where, with any luck, I hoped to get fresh camels to carry us on to the next stage.

Soon it became apparent that all camels attract flies and camels with festering sores attract more than most. The hindquarters of the beasts were covered with large, flat-bodied creatures that promptly transferred their attention to my bare legs.

Little antelopes bounced into the scrub as if on springs. Remembering that I had to provide the men with meat it was some comfort to know that we should be within the boundaries of a reserve for at least another ten miles. On the first day out I wanted to conceal the fact that I knew almost nothing about how to use a rifle.

Hours passed before we reached the mountains and began to walk in the shadow of the Ol Conto pass. The camels shambled along like carthorses and I saw no good reason why we should not carry on until we got within sight of a suitable camping place.

Lelean thought otherwise. He made it clear that we ought to halt to adjust the loads. He wanted to get through the pass by nightfall because we were in elephant country and, as I learned to my cost later on, a good camel leader steers clear of elephants. We halted for about a quarter of an hour, which gave me an opportunity to look at the men more closely.

Among a motley of local unemployed, five were on my payroll. They worked; the others leaned on their spears and watched them. Lelean, my headman, was the most active of all. With his black, close-cropped head and bustling manner he looked like a bumble bee buzzing from camel to camel, testing load-ropes, readjusting the wooden supports of the harness and talking to everyone. Karo, the man who had carried off the rope trick, seemed to be getting in his way and I wondered how long it would be before there was trouble between them.

When we stopped for a second time, the sun burned down high and

Obstacle course

bright. I felt as fresh as they come, but I became a little anxious about
the track. The Ol Conto had narrowed to a defile with steep sides,
overhung with black rock: oppressive country by any reckoning. No
sound except for an occasional echoing cough from the baboons on the
hillside. Overhead an eagle hung like a cross nailed to the sky.

The track got worse. What worried me was the absence of any
appreciable slope. We reached the lip of the cliff after ambling along
for some hours. Suddenly, as if curtains had been swept aside, we
seemed to be looking over the edge of the world. Fascinated as I was I
became morbidly conscious that somehow twelve men, seven camels
and 1,800 pounds of baggage had to be inched down the side of a cliff.

During the descent I winced each time I heard an agonised roar
from the camels above, that is, whenever their spindly legs and heavily
cushioned feet became jammed between boulders. Most of the hangers-
on began to scramble back, but on Lelean's advice I retained two of
the toughest at a shilling a head to act as road-makers on the way down.
Munta, the man with wife trouble back in Wamba, got us out of some
of the worst of our difficulties.

Dawn on safari

On one fearful occasion a camel mounted a ramp, swayed precariously at the top and fell into an unseen hole below. It remained upright, suspended by its load, but its legs appeared to be pinned in a narrow crack between two slabs of rock. The creature bellowed piteously, the more so because the men thrashed it from behind and hauled on a head-rope that was already stained with frothy blood. Munta strove to get beneath the animal. By tugging on a twisted leg and shoving under its massive breast-bone, he induced the camel to rise unsteadily. But only on three legs. It looked as if the knee of the forelimb had been crushed. I wondered if I would have to shoot the animal and, if so, whether it would be better to use the shotgun or the rifle. Eventually we took off its load and towed it along.

Towards sundown Lelean pointed to a green patch some hundreds of yards below, where a small plateau led into a subsidiary valley. He thought we might camp there, and the last incident of the day occurred when we were within sight of camp and mindful only of food and rest.

I thought we had found an excellent place to camp, but Lelean seemed anxious, first because there was no browse for the camels and second, and more ominously, because he had noticed an abundance of elephant droppings under the trees. Suddenly he stopped, lifted his finger and looked at me. A metallic call of *tek-tek-tek* came from the bushes beneath the trees. He had heard guinea fowl. As I fumbled for a cartridge, Lelean slipped off behind the trees to drive the birds out into the open, where I should be able to catch them on the wing. Events thereafter became somewhat confused.

Lelean disappeared. The twittering ceased. I pulled the safety catch forwards and crept towards the tallest tree, but instead of the expected flutter of birds, a big bull elephant strode out of the bushes. It saw me; it raised its trunk and screamed shrilly. There was no mistaking its intention. It was scared and it promptly turned and made off.

If the elephant was scared, the camel standing half undressed among a mound of gear was terrified. It reared up and rushed off towards the far side of the dry river-bed with a length of rope and a box trailing from one leg. At a point where it tried to climb out of the gulley it tripped and fell over.

Karo pulled the rope clear of its thrashing legs, but though it repeatedly jerked its neck up in the air, not even Munta could make it stand up. Watching where he lightly massaged the animal, I gathered that if a bone was not actually broken, the shoulder had been badly sprained.

In camp that night, the first of nearly a hundred I spent in the bush, I was too tired to write more than fragmentary notes in my diary. It became an inventory of first experiences, ending '. . . encountered elephant, much gear broken, one camel lame, one probably crippled and one day done.'

ORDEAL BY COMBAT

Mezek, my young Turkana cook and houseboy, woke me up gently at six o'clock with a pot of tea. I returned his greetings and listened without much attention to a story only half understood. It sounded as if the camels had run away during the night. I stared at him incredulously.

'*Run away! Where?*'

He shrugged his shoulders and repeated that they had gone. As he didn't seem very worried, I slipped on a pair of shorts and strolled out into the camp lines with no sense of urgency. For days I had thought about little except camels. I should not have been unduly surprised to learn that at least one couldn't stand up. Instead they had run away. Doubtless we should find them or someone would bring them back. That's the way things happened on safari.

Lelean related briefly what had happened. The animals had been penned up in a *boma* built out of prickly thorn scrub. Because they were tired and two were lame they had not been hobbled. At one point in the fence they had eaten their way out. Perhaps they were scared by the almost incessant howling of hyenas. Five were missing; the two sick beasts were still squatting down, dribbling and mooing, miserably, like cows. By pattering his fingers on his arms he indicated that two men were still running after the fugitives. Clearly an occasion for a dressing down, but I could think of nothing better to say than, '*Iko m'baya sana sana.*' That is bad, very bad. But when the beasts were returned, looking better after a free midnight feast, I said it with no special conviction. Life on the whole was unexpectedly good. I ate breakfast of cold guinea fowl, lit a cheroot and gave the order to move.

By eleven o'clock we had covered about ten miles. The going was irksome rather than arduous. We slouched over a plain dotted with little prickly bushes rather like low gorse. The prickles raised a network of scratches around my bare ankles and I was obliged to hop and skip in the manner of a Scottish reel. This amused the men and irritated me.

During the afternoon we came across an immense caravan, Samburu moving towards their dry-season grazing grounds on the Losai Hills. The tribesmen were accompanied by more cattle, sheep and goats than I had ever seen before. A few camels jogged along, but they were not the kind I should have cared to hire, even to supplement our own; they were scrawny beasts, emaciated by the loss of blood which is drawn from them once a week and drunk mixed with milk. Each family walked beside its own donkeys, to which they had lashed everything lashable.

In these panniers babies howled, goats bleated and puppies yapped. All the inmates were trussed like chickens. When I tried to take a photograph of living cargo mixed up with mats and cooking pots, the indignant father dragged the donkey along so fast that I feared for the safety of the child's wildly wobbling head. The caravan swept on with a disturbing sense of urgency over endless plains, stumbling in cracked earth, ringed by flat horizons only.

The Samburu are a curious people. Closely related to the Masai in almost everything, especially hypertrophy of the ego, they are exceptionally good-looking, arrogant and lazy. Condemned to a life of incessant wandering, they take their leisure seriously, existing for days on the principle of least effort. When I met the Samburu alone I sometimes had the impression that they were staring at me, but their eyes showed that they were staring forwards, and I just happened to be in the way.

We began to look for a camping site about four o'clock in the afternoon. As it was becoming cooler and I had become adept at skipping over acacia bushes, I wanted to march on for at least another hour, but Lelean had his mind on the camels. He emphasised that one was sick, another lame and all of them 'wanted to *lala*'. This seemed insufficient reason for a halt of more than a few minutes, but feeling that I might have misunderstood him, I looked the word up. It means 'to rest or sleep'.

The best place for a *lala* seemed to be a patch of bare ground about the size of a football pitch. As it was almost entirely surrounded by prickly scrub, I wondered whether it might not perhaps be too bare. It looked like the sort of place where we should find rhinoceroses, or those diabolical insects, warrior ants, known locally as *siafu*, the killers. I left the men to it and went for a stroll. When they started to erect the tents they stirred up a colony of these ants, and I returned to find noisy confusion; after two further attempts we gave up and pitched camp among some acacia bushes. They might scratch, but they couldn't bite.

No doubt aided and abetted by the ever guileful Karo, Lelean was clearly up to something. On the highly improbable grounds that the camel scared by the elephant had scattered the men's *posho* they were *ukosefu sana*, very hungry. Determined not to let them pull that one again, I called for a *baraza*, a public pow-wow.

They lined up. I gave each man seven pounds of *posho*, two pounds of sugar, a quarter of a pound of tea and a small portion of fat, enough in all to last a week. Thereafter they should look after themselves. Did they want anything else?

An idiotic question. They wanted more food. Not just additives. They had to work hard. More than anything they wanted some vegetables and by vegetables (*m'boga*) they meant good meat which they could add to their dreary diet of *posho*. They reminded me that I'd said I'd give them at least one animal a week.

'No animals here,' I said firmly. Another stupid remark. Lelean had cunningly chosen a site where there was an abundance of game. Everyone – everyone, that is, except me – had seen a small family of Grant's

gazelles on a nearby hill besides some elands and zebras. I put the field *Surprised elephant*
glasses down and nodded sadly. Clearly I had been pushed into the
vegetable-shooting business. I take no pleasure in recalling subsequent
events.

It took about a quarter of an hour to get within 400 yards of the
gazelles. Lelean loped ahead with my rifle, Karo followed with the
shotgun and a sharp *panga*. I did my best to keep up with them. Both
men crouched as they ran, but seemed quite unconcerned by the fact

that the animals had spotted us. We reached a straggly acacia, the only substantial piece of cover within sight. Lelean handed me the rifle. '*Piga*! *Piga*! Shoot quickly,' he said.

I shook my head. The range of about 300 yards was far beyond my competence. The high-speed Winchester 30.06 had been zeroed at a hundred yards on a range in North London before I left for Africa. With a little bit of lift and a lot of luck I might have brought it down at about 200. Whatever happened during the rest of the safari I was anxious to hit something with my first shot. 'Too far. No good,' I said.

The men looked so disappointed that I crawled down a gulley to about 150 yards. Telling the men to wait, I pulled back the safety catch and set off on a distinctly uncomfortable stalk.

I had my eye on a big buck with a fine pair of horns. By poking the rifle through the lower branches of a bush I reckoned that I should be able to hit it in the shoulder. Putting on my spectacles I peered at the

Samburu hut

animal. It seemed blurred and curiously distorted. My glasses were

misty. More fiddling about. I cleaned them; I got the buck in the sights for the second time and squeezed. Nothing happened. Dreadful feeling. I had forgotten to release the safety catch. In pushing it forwards I made a slight noise. The buck slewed round until it was facing me.

I squeezed again. Tremendous crash. My glasses fell off and from the puff of dust I realised that my shot had gone wide by about two feet. The animals promptly plunged off into the bush.

Lelean ran up excited and somewhat indignant, explaining in Swahili, rapidly, difficult to understand, that one should approach animals obliquely, lie down and shoot on the spot, no stalking.

The gazelles were still within sight, so I handed him the rifle. He missed four times and emptied the magazine. It looked as if the vegetable problem could be resolved only by competitive target practice.

That night I pinned four pages of my notebook on to a tree with thorns and we hammered away at it, four shots each at a hundred paces. After correcting for a bad miss I got three inner. From that I learned that bullets carried in an unprotected magazine under very hot sun fly high when fired, because of vastly increased muzzle velocity.

Thereafter from a known angle of correction I usually got bang on target, while Lelean didn't hit the tree once. In addition to his other responsibilities, *B'wana* became the provider of vegetables.

That evening four brace of guinea fowl knocked off on our way back to camp away from those insidious ants vastly improved staff relationships.

THE SAMBURU WOMAN

At the end of the third day it was obvious that the injured camel could no longer keep up with us. It lurched about like a drunk and when it fell down it found it difficult to get up.

Munta the camel man was gentle with the sick animal. Instead of giving it a clout with a stick or a kick on the hindquarters as the other men did, he talked it into rising and helped it with a push from the rear. No good. In the end it had to be shot, dissected and sun-dried for rations.

Thereupon Munta left us too. The woman at Wamba was still on his mind. Holding up three fingers he indicated that in three days he would be back where no red-painted rival could slip in unawares. Predictably, Karo offered to stand in as syce until I could get another camel leader.

That night I was obliged to display my meagre knowledge of medicine. It was about eight o'clock. The light of our huge fire had attracted little groups of Samburu from the adjacent *manyatta*. What I did not know was that Lelean had procured a large goat on the strength of my unproven skill as a medicine man. When I had finished dinner he brought a herdsman to the door of my tent. The man, he said, was 'very sick'. I tried to remember my homework.

'The sickness it is where?'

The man sighed and stroked his body from his forehead to his navel.

This was discouraging. I flicked over the pages of a dictionary, looking for the word for 'pain'. It was *uma*, which also meant thorn, lightning and penis.

'Have you a fork in your head?'

He shook his head.

'In your chest?'

No forks there.

'In your belly?'

His face brightened. Holding his hands over his bare stomach, he opened and closed his fingers spasmodically. He was transfixed with forks. 'Many, many,' he said. They were biting and clawing at him. They were very bad. He had had them for three days. Suspecting worms, I tried another tack.

'Much lavatory?'

He shook his head violently.

'No lavatory?'

He nodded and began a ludicrous mime in crouching position which made it abundantly clear that he was suffering from acute constipation. I gave him enough cascara to worm a camel.

Four cases of diarrhoea received kaolin; the headaches got an aspirin each; I gave two sulpha tablets to an old man with many forks in his chest and much coughing, while daubs of iodine sufficed for superficial cuts and scratches.

My last case was a woman called Malaya. She was of such outstanding beauty that I was rather taken aback when she sauntered into the little halo of yellow light from the oil lamp. I say sauntered because in her movements there was something of the casual grace of the trained mannequin. The illusion was heightened by her theatrical investment in a piece of cloth which was wrapped tightly round her thighs and fell in classical folds round her ankles. Apart from jewellery it was all she wore: the Malaya was copper-coloured, straight as a reed and bare from the waist upwards. The symmetry of her conical breasts was emphasised by the curved shadow of an enormous necklet of woven wire that hung over her shoulders. Her arms were held limply, but like a ballet dancer the fingers were curved as if to emphasise her figure. Lelean brought her forward, but instead of saying what was the matter with her as he had done with the others, he whispered, 'She is a Malaya,' and gave the impression that there had been an argument about whether this woman had any right to join in the queue of patients.

Malaya: the whore

For a moment or two she looked at me without speaking. Then she said she wanted medicine – not ordinary medicine but powerful *dawa*, 'to bring a child'.

Not knowing what to say and feeling somewhat disconcerted about the whole business of quackery, I fobbed her off with a couple of bright red vitamin tablets. It was not until I asked questions about the girl the next day that I learned that *malaya* meant whore. A woman known to be barren had no other gainful occupation.

Moon Over the Matthews

Ahead of us the place where I hoped to pick up some more camels began to flash in the sun, but far from being the spectacular town I had imagined from the bottom of the valley, it was a drab collection of mud huts on the top of a ridge of cinders in front of which camels eventually flopped down. The daub walls of the *duka*, the local store, had crumbled to such an extent that the proprietor had patched them up with sheets of tin that flashed like a heliograph. Seen against a background of palm trees and distant hills, the squalor was somehow improbable, and so too was our arrival: I had the feeling of being irrelevant to our surroundings. It was as if we had been at sea for a long time and no longer cared whether we reached a long-sought harbour.

Karo had sidled up to me the previous day with the complaint that his blanket was threadbare at the point where it covered his backside. My recollection was that he normally wore a somewhat dilapidated pair of shorts, but he insisted that he had nothing else to wear and, as he put it, he wanted to walk without shame among the people of Rodosoit. I made the ridiculous mistake of giving him one of my own pairs. Within five minutes Lelean turned up with a similar story. He said he had worn out his government issue in my service and could he please have what I had given Karo. When Goiti and Mezek appeared on the scene I didn't wait to hear their story, but promised everyone a new pair, emphasising that it would be the last they would get from me. The lesson cost me thirty-seven shillings.

The proprietor of the *duka* was a thin-faced Somali, smooth and black as a stick of licorice, who seemed to be cut off from his customers by a barricade of skinny bosoms. They belonged to the tribal matriarchs who leaned over the counter with arms folded and discussed the gossip of the day.

Stretching over the barricade of bosoms I asked for drinks all round for my men. They preferred Pepsi-cola to tinned beer.

Going well   The Somali was smarter than I thought. Interpreting my order in its

widest sense he gave a bottle to every man in the store and told me I owed him thirty shillings. Another minor defeat.

After buying a gallon of paraffin and six tin mugs which can be used for almost anything on safari, I walked out of the back door of the *duka* to find eight little camels browsing contentedly on straw from an old mattress. They were the reinforcements from Marsabit. I stared at them for several minutes and with more pleasure than I can easily describe; they were good animals by any reckoning but by comparison with our own string of cripples, they were fit to carry the wares of the Prophet, who knew a thing or two about camels.

At Rodosoit we were joined by three new men: Aboud, the syce who had driven the camels in, and two game scouts, one called Lengama – who was as thick as a brick – and Lenduroni, a short stocky fellow with a studious manner. He alone of the company seemed to be aware of the world outside the desert; he asked me questions about Nairobi. He wanted to know if there was much game in my country and what he could expect to earn if he walked to England. He was a hard worker and applied himself to a new problem by wrinkling up his forehead like a dachshund before suggesting what was usually an original solution.

With a staff of seven I soon had a superb camp on the banks of a dried-up stream. We had almost everything we wanted: two pools of clear water, browse for the camels, an abundance of shade and the *duka* on the hilltop that might have passed for the village pub. My tent nestled under a tree where the bushes were cut back to make a screen for a field bathroom. Beyond the tent, conveniently shaded, the sprawling limbs of a fallen tree provided a gun rack, a hat stand and pegs for clothing. I lounged contentedly in the crook of its limbs with a ledge for books above and a place for tea-things below. This was comfort on a scale rarely experienced in the bush.

Towards dusk the high road of the stream-bed was used by little groups of red-daubed boys, striding out towards the grove for the circumcision ceremony. They took immense strides; they carried spears and chanted in unison. The loud chorus was interrupted by individual solos of *Ah ya ikoto! Ah yah!* Whether in that final, explosive, almost agonised *Ah yah!* there was sympathetic magic calculated to relieve the pain from the inexpertly used headman's knife, I cannot say. The boys were tense and purposive and Karo and Lelean teased them as they strode by. They took up the *Ah ya ikoto*, and made a downward chopping gesture with their hands.

The novitiates scarcely looked at their tormentors. There was no slackening of their exaggerated stride. They had an appointment with manhood. *Ah ya!*

At six o'clock that night Karo shouted something loud and incomprehensible from the far end of the camp. It sounded like '*Swara! Swara!*' He began to run towards Lelean, who was cleaning my rifle. Lelean looked up, threw down the ramrod and ran towards me. '*Swara!*' he repeated, pointing urgently towards the bush. Lengama called to Mezek; Lenduroni was already trotting along beside Karo. The situation was completely out of hand. I had the feeling that we were about to be attacked.

'*Swara*, it is what?' I said, panting behind Lelean. We were some fifty yards from the camp before I learnt that it was a *nyama*, that is, some kind of animal.

'A fierce one?'

In imagination I saw a troop of frenzied elephants, hysterical rhinos, maybe a lion. But the word for elephant I knew was *n'dovu*, rhino was *faro*, lion *simba*. What were *swara*?

Lelean was somewhat non-committal. After admitting that it was an animal 'for food' he held his arms over his head like horns. *Swara* was none other than my old friend Grant's gazelle. It was about 300 yards away and walking proudly, like a heraldic stag.

I tried to remember the lessons taught by the target practice with sheets of my notebook and all I'd been told by my instructor in London. I stiffened. A drop of sweat ran down my forehead. At a point about 150 yards from us, the animal stopped and lifted up its head.

I fired.

The thump seemed in no sense related to the explosion in the breech. I had no recollection of the physical recoil of the rifle. I was conscious only of a spasm almost sexual in its intensity. Even before I squeezed I felt as if the animal were already dead. The gazelle collapsed gently, like a coat that had slipped off a coat-hanger.

At nine o'clock that night the moon rose above the topmost peak of Ol Doino Lengiyo. Against the velvet backcloth of the night it resembled a crescentic knife. I thought of the ritual mutilation and of the boys who sang as they strode out for their painful appointment with manhood. *Ah ya!*

The Red Elephants

Days later we swung into the broad, dry stream-bed of the Milgis only to find the *lugga* populated by a herd of most unusual-looking elephants; they were brick-red, the result of dusting themselves with dry earth. My instinct was to swing out again and leave them to it, but the map showed clearly that somehow we had to cross that *lugga*. It ran at right angles to our course and stood between us and the N'doto Hills.

The elephants seemed quite unaware of our presence. However, a slight shift in the direction of the wind would envelop us in the scent of elephant and that, as I had discovered, was enough to terrify the camels. All the obvious crossing points had been recently used by elephants. Some of the animals were still standing in the shade of the trees on the opposite bank and it was not difficult to imagine that they were standing there *waiting*.

Lenduroni found a good place to cross. The bank had caved in; the slope was gentle and with the red earth up to their knees the camels lurched down into the stream-bed. There were no elephants within sight, but it soon appeared that it was no easier to get out of the stream-bed than it had been to get in, and we were obliged to trudge up the Milgis for several miles.

When we eventually ran into the trouble I had anticipated I was at the end of the convoy trying to take a photograph. The leading camel suddenly started to rear; eventually broke free, releasing the second camel, and panic set in. One animal shed part of its load and raced off down the *lugga*, the leading animal tried to mount the distant bank but became bogged down in soft earth, and two others fled upstream. The cause of the trouble was an old bull elephant who rose above us with the dignity of a colossus hewn out of stone.

It took us the better part of the day to reassemble the caravan. The stampede cost me two bottles of Scotch, a little petroleum stove and a lamp; my shaving mirror was cracked; the collapsible chair collapsed and about half a sack of maize and thirty pounds of rice were scattered. A wooden box containing water-purifying equipment and biological collecting gear was never found.

We pitched camp above the Milgis where I shot my second animal, a gerenuk, an extremely slender relative of the gazelle. Rapidly aiming at the nearest animal, I fired and was disappointed to see it lower itself as if to resume feeding on the ground. The other two skewed round, startled, unsure where the crash of the shot had come from. As I pushed the bolt forwards for a second attempt, to my surprise the animal I had aimed at slumped to the ground. Although shot through the heart it had remained standing for several seconds.

That night we had about a dozen Samburu as guests for dinner. Lengama the Muslim complained that he couldn't eat an animal unless it had first had its throat slit, so I owed him the cost of a meal, but I'm pretty sure he ate his portion when he thought nobody was looking. In the N'doto Hills we were rarely without guides or hangers-on, and reciprocal hospitality began to develop into rounds of feasts.

Advance guard   One night I managed to chase a hyena – not out of but into my tent.

The only casualty was a canvas shoe suspended above my bed. The animal bit off the toecap as cleanly as if it had been sliced off with a pair of shears and I wondered if my foot would have had the same treatment had I been wearing the shoe. The incident started when, hearing hyenas call with growing insistence, I shone the torch and saw two or three pairs of bright green eyes. I threw a brick and chased them off. Walking back I saw one animal disappear through the back flap. Apparently I had chased it through, and thought later there was much to be said for leaving a tent open at both ends.

To reach South Horr on our last day in the N'dotos we had to march for ten hours through a beautiful valley where we found the smallest camel I have seen.

The calf had been born during the night; the stringy little cord was still bright red and the animal had some difficulty in standing up. The mother wore a seraphic expression. When the men approached she pranced in front of the new-born and licked it vigorously.

After some talk among themselves, the men cut some hefty cudgels from a tree and advanced on the mother animal. Lelean gave her a smart blow on the hindquarters; Karo poked at her muzzle with a stick and when she shied away from her calf, Aboud, the strongest man in the company, grabbed the little animal and hoisted it on to his shoulders like a yoke. Holding the calf's spindly legs under his arms, he began to run. Everyone began to run, including the anxious cow. I ran too, although I didn't know why we were running or what they intended to do with the calf. 'Simana!' I shouted. 'Simana!' Stop! Stop!

The explanation was more simple than I could have imagined. Far from carrying off the calf, the men were trying to return both it and its mother to their rightful owners. From the earmark they had seen that the pair belonged to a nearby band of Samburu. As it would have been difficult to drive both animals, they decided to carry the calf until they could leave it at the mouth of the valley near the main track across the plain where they knew the mother would follow and both animals would soon be found. Once again I was impressed by the Africans' respect for one another's property. But not wild animals. When a giraffe – a protected animal not on my licence – peered at us, they all implored me to shoot it.

THE WIND AND THE STARS

Apart from the fact that the forestry station at South Horr clung to the side of a mountain, it had almost everything I associated with the word

Eight hours old

oasis – fresh air, burbling water, rustling trees including eucalyptus and acacia, but also olives, leathery-leaved evergreens and a sprinkling of flame trees acuiver with sunbirds. The village stood in the gap between the towering walls of N'yiru and the Ol Doino Mara. It is the narrow gateway to Lake Rudolf and the highway south for the tribes who live at the southern end of the lake. With any luck we should reach Lake Rudolf within two or three days.

A government *askari*, incongruously got up in a khaki cap, a red blanket and army boots, walked up with a visitor's book containing questions about where we had come from, where we were going and why. I shook my head. We were on safari. To hell with documentation. The *askari* looked worried. To keep him happy I wrote something facetious across the top of the page. He saluted and walked off. I wondered who was responsible for the book and when he last inspected it. Among the names of the more improbable visitors to South Horr recently had been Julius Caesar, Nikita Khrushchev and Ella Wheeler Wilcox.

In less time than it took to unpack the medicine chest we were surrounded by tall, red-painted men and their wives and girlfriends. One of the most endearing qualities of the Samburu is the affection they bestow on their womenfolk. Bantu treat their women as beasts of burden. I had become accustomed to the sight of Kikuyu girls staggering along under immense loads of firewood, some with a baby peering out from amongst it, like a nestling, while their husbands swaggered along disdaining to carry anything more than a spear. This is never seen among the Samburu, who are proud of their aristocratic-looking wives.

Despite his years Goiti disappeared with a saucy-looking piece on the first night and forgot to hobble two of the camels, which wandered off and had to be driven back, roaring loudly, at two o'clock in the morning. Perhaps they had a date of their own.

The men usually slept out in the open, spreading mosquito nets over their heads. With large holes burnt in them by sparks from the fire, this flimsy protection was of no use against flies, but it was some insurance against hyenas or other animals and there were rarely mosquitos to be contended with.

As a sign of class distinction, Lelean rarely slept among the men and at South Horr he went to enormous lengths to build a seraglio among the branches of a fallen tree. This was his bachelor apartment and he was rarely without a woman there throughout the whole of the next day. The interior was voluptuously furnished with mats laid over ammunition boxes; the bait was a continually boiling kettle of tea. Some women drifted to his bower from the sick parade; he waited until they had been treated and then invited them in for tea. I was alarmed to find that cases with pleurisy and skin disease were using my crockery

and told him to use his own. I noticed that he entertained two or three women at the same time. Quite a man.

Here the problem was the old one of trying to keep troops up to scratch under luxury conditions. There was much to be done in the way of repairing wear and tear and to get it done I had to draw up a roster and ban strangers who came into camp for tea and gossip. When I announced that it was time for us to go, I was met with a distinct lack of enthusiasm from the entire company and of course they all had lists of plausible excuses.

As I stumped back to my tent wondering what to do next, a bird jeered at me and another one chuckled throatily. The noise came from a group of starlings gorgeously got up in metallic greens and golds. As at Wamba I was somewhat apprehensive about being to so great an extent self-dependent. On similar occasions I have found that nothing puts the black dog of melancholy to flight more quickly than a conscientious bout of bird-watching, butterfly-observing or spying on nature in general. Carrying the gun and a pair of field glasses I strode off into the forest on my own.

The belief that tropical forests are rich in birds and flowers may be justified in some parts of the world. In the Congo and certainly in East Africa the high forests are disappointing places. The evident drama of this forest was confined to the stream, seen in the cold poise of a leaf-green mantis or the diamond head of a water snake protruding above the surface of a pool.

Local gossips

Samburu chief

During the talk around the fireside that night I heard the word *upepo* mentioned again and again. It meant wind, the great wind that roared westwards from beyond Mount Kulal and thrashed the shores of the lake. As there was a light wind blowing at the time, I began to wonder what the morning might bring and whether we should be able to reach the lake by dusk.

The morning was hot, bright and scarcely breezy. At high noon when we strode out of the shadow of the palms, the heights of Pel danced in the heat.

We walked for about four miles before I began to understand the topography of the gap. The symmetry was such that the mountain flanks on either side disappeared into the distance like railway lines. The topmost tip of Kulal was just visible ahead, but with every step we took it seemed to rise a little from the floor of the lava below the crest of the escarpment.

The heat became intense. Apart from observing with monotonous regularity that there were 'forks in the sun', the men said very little. Goiti urged the camels forward with a throaty '*Hodai!*' repeated at intervals. I never discovered what *hodai* meant, if indeed it meant anything. And Goiti soon tired of saying it. So I talked to my own camel, 'the little white one'.

Shortly before sundown we marched over a ridge and looked down on a lunar landscape of lava. It stretched out into infinity. Although the hot wind blew against us gently, everything was uncannily still and I had the impression that we alone were alive in a dead world. There was not even a drop of water in the Anderi *lugga*. This was not a serious matter as we carried an emergency supply of four gallons. There were said to be one or two permanent water-holes immediately ahead of us and at worst we could march through the night to the lake, which was marked on the map as 'brackish but drinkable'.

Lake Rudolf, or the Jade Sea as I called it, was discovered on 6 March 1888 by the Austrian Count Teleki von Sek. He was an interesting man who had made an ambitious foot safari across almost the whole of East Africa, accompanied by three Swahilis, six guides, eight Somalis, fifteen *askaris*, over 200 porters and his faithful, plodding, dull-witted biographer, Lt Ludwig von Hohnel. What little we know of the count himself comes through the laborious and sycophantic prose of the lieutenant, poured out in two large volumes.

I used half my water allocation that night on a brew of tea. There was not enough for a wash and I was not prepared to wash my hands and face in camel urine as the boys did.

As I sat on my canvas chair sipping tea, everything seemed to resolve itself into the absence of water. I had made a bad mistake in not setting out with more than an emergency supply. It would not have happened if I had paid more attention to the map and less to gossip . The water in the Anderi was up in the hills and not where we had crossed the *lugga*. It would have been better if we had camped in the stream-bed and sent out a party to look for the well. So I made poor jokes (in Swahili) about loading the camels that morning.

To the Jade Sea

The wind began to rise at dawn until at times it had some of the skull-wrinkling intensity of a scream. The hot blast of air might have come from a furnace. When the thorn trees shrilled and sand began to pile up against my pillow, I had no desire to do anything except stay precisely where I was, curled up under a dirty brown sheet on the ground. It seemed as if the expedition had come to a dead stop before we even reached the lake. In fact if the men had not been so cheerful about the wind I might have ordered a smart counter-march back to the South Horr valley. Yet Mezek seemed to think it funny when a gush of precious tea was carried away like spume before it reached the cup; Lelean conceded that the *upepo* was very bad but he thought it would soon die down and Karo laughed uproariously when my sheet blew away. He bounded after it whooping and cheering. This did me a lot of good.

When we began to lumber forward at nine o'clock I got some comfort from the thought that if we could put up with the hard going until midday it was unlikely that we should find conditions much worse anywhere else.

At this point in the journey I felt both apprehensive and jubilant. Apprehensive for obvious reasons; jubilant because I felt physically competent to walk as far as the camels would take us. My feet were tougher than they had ever been before, largely due to Thesiger's advice about wearing canvas shoes. It was the best I could have had. The men wore their variations of Somali sandals made out of pieces of discarded tyres. Among the lava the straps broke and they pulled out the tacks with their teeth, hammering the strips together with a stone.

Lelean was concerned about the haze ahead of us. He said it was a very bad sandstorm and indicated that we should avoid it if we could. Although it streamed along some two or three miles to our left the corridor of blown sand looked dense and suffocating. Dust devils scurried towards us and I was relieved when the haze veered away, but two camels became hysterical.

I had made a singularly bad attempt at taking a cross-bearing on two distant peaks. Far from being the mountain I thought it was, one

133

All in together

The cruelest bit

Little white one

Midday break

turned out to be a little pimple of rock on a distant mound of lava and the other slowly disappeared like the Cheshire Cat until only the fragments remained suspended in the sky. It looked as if it had exploded; it was in fact only a mirage.

The midday halt brought us to a place where the lava had been ground down to powder by rare floods of the Balessa Kulal, a *lugga* which rose in the Chalbi Desert and ran for eighty or ninety miles roughly parallel to the east shore of the lake behind Mount Kulal.

Under a bush in the *lugga* Lelean located a sleeping naked Turkana fisherman, one of the tallest and thinnest men I have ever seen. He put me in mind of a black sand eel. His name was either Ekali or Ekairu. I remember him as the Indolent Ikky and although I have a poor sense of smell it was apparent that Ikky, his camel and almost everything about him stank like a box of ferrets. He had been fishing in the lake and his catch, which looked like long ribbons of haddock, was hung about the bush to dry. It was covered in flies and so was Ikky. But he was fast asleep, lost in whatever the Turkana dream about.

We stood round him for a moment without speaking and then Lelean greeted him in Swahili. No response. Mezek repeated the salutation in Turkana. Ikky continued to snore. At this Karo, with a delicacy which did him credit, put a little pinch of dust into the sleeper's broad nostrils. Ikky awoke explosively and reached for his spear.

Mezek assured him that we were peacefully inclined and merely wanted to share the *lugga* with him ('we friends'). He then explained to us that Ikky was on his way to a nearby *manyatta* with a load of fish and fresh water from a local spring.

At the word water I brightened up considerably. Ikky carried about twelve gallons in the goatskin *baromels* slung over his camel. No doubt he would be prepared to make a second journey to the well. Would he accept five shillings for the water?

'*Shilingi tano kwa maji*,' I said to Mezek, but before it could be translated into Turkana Lelean rounded on me with a furious 'No! No!' My inability to bargain with people and the ease with which they got the better of me inspired him with an angry compassion. He was as close-fisted with my money as he was with his own. In Swahili he gave me to understand that the man was only a damned nigger (*M'shenzi meusi*) and would probably part with whatever he had for a handful of tobacco.

In this he was mistaken, for neither money, tobacco nor tea appeared to be of the slightest interest to the self-sufficient Ikky. What he wanted, he said, was *argri* – and *argri*, I knew, was meat. After chewing at the end of a fatty piece of dried camel meat he nodded reluctantly, as if implying that it was indeed edible – something I was inclined to doubt – but what he really wanted was fresh meat and he leered, smacking his lips and pointing to my rifle.

Depressing suggestion. I had hoped there would be no more shooting until we reached the lake, and we hadn't seen a gazelle since we left Anderi. I shook my head. Mezek said, 'No meat here,' and Lelean turned his back on the man in feigned disgust.

'*Mom?*' said Ikky incredulously. '*Mom?* What! No meat?' He sprang to his feet with surprising agility and began to speak rapidly to Mezek. It seemed that even as the man slept he had heard the explosive whistle of a nearby duiker. He thought the little antelope was somewhere among the bushes on the far side of the *lugga*. No doubt it was still there and if it was he could find it and I could shoot it. *Mom?*

Cursing the need for both food and water I followed the naked Turkana into the bush with Lengama and Lelean following on behind. Ikky could have out-tracked a pack of police dogs. He never hurried. He kept his eyes on the ground and gave the impression of a dull but diligent child slowly reading aloud from a primer.

After a leisurely stroll up and down the *lugga* we (that is to say Ikky) picked up the little hoofprints of the duiker in a bed of sand scarcely a hundred yards from where he had slept. He showed us where the animal had paused, turned round and defecated. We followed it up one bank of a gulley and back down the other side. The spoor was plain enough *Feared sand storm*

in the sand, but how Ikky kept on its track when it moved over stony ground was beyond my comprehension. I suspect that given the general direction from points in the sand he anticipated where it was likely to go and kept on moving backwards and forwards until he picked up the trail again.

We found the duiker on a knoll among a troop of baboons which began to bark and run away. The duiker ran too, like a bouncing ball. At the time my attitude towards shooting was still unresolved, for describing the incident in my notebook later I wrote:

> Got it slap on the head first shot. Head disappeared. Damn all shooting. Why damn? Who ate the animal? We all ate a bit of it. . . . Scarcely anything left of the duiker. The Turkana ran the guts through his fingers before wolfing something which looked like undigested grass in the stomach. Seems to be a local delicacy. Looked horrible.

When Mezek walked up with a large pot of tea I discovered that either Lelean was in league with the Turkana or I had completely misunderstood the long-winded argument about exchanging meat for water. There was a water-hole in the *lugga*. During our absence the boys had

Hysteria among camels

Camel revolts

filled up four jerry cans with a clear but slightly salty liquid. This came as such a surprise that I spluttered indignantly when I tried to find out why it had been necessary to shoot the duiker. In up-country Swahili the past tense is indicated by the word *nakwisha*, literally 'I finish': this seems to make nonsense of most verbs, especially those used in the negative. To make matters worse there is no Swahili word for 'to have'. One is 'with something' or, negatively, 'not with it'.

When he grasped what I was talking about, Lelean said that of course he knew about the water. What did I imagine had brought the duiker and the baboons into the *lugga*? Everybody knew about the water in Balessa Kulal. As for the duiker, we had shot it because the Turkana hadn't eaten meat for a long time. As everyone needed meat it was necessary for us to give him some.

I looked hard for signs of deceit in his dark brown eyes, but finding none I concluded that on this, as on other occasions, there was more than a little self-interest in the remarkable hospitality of one African to another. Thesiger tells a story about a Bedu Sheikh who was known as the Host of the Wolves because whenever he heard a wolf howl around his tent at night he ordered his son to take a goat into the desert, saying that he would have no one call on him for dinner in vain.

The clouds of blown sand began to disappear during the afternoon and, hoping the worst was over for the day, I ordered the camels to be loaded. The order was received with marked apathy but I wanted to be within sight of the lake before nightfall. I watched them as they became part of the horizon.

With the indolent Ikky as a guide we left the shelter of the *lugga* only to discover that the wind was still blowing like an express train. As we marched towards the Longippi Hills, Kulal, away to the north, began to rise to a formidable height. From the top of a pile of dirty brown rocks honeycombed with bubbles like the fossilised foam of a sewer, I searched the land with field glasses for a long-anticipated glimpse of the lake. Beyond Longippi the hills were a smoky violet colour, and Lelean assured me they were 'among the homes of the Turkana'. This meant that they rose from the western shore of Rudolf and that the lake, although still invisible, was somewhere in the hollow ahead of us. At any moment I expected to catch a flash of bright water.

What did catch my eye was a row of cairns ahead, each about twelve feet in diameter at the base and so regular in shape that they alone seemed real among the unrealities of the landscape. Neumann the elephant hunter had seen the stone circles seventy years earlier and 'thought they must have formed the ground plan of some sort of rude huts'. But, as he said, 'Who had made them or what they should have been doing in that desert and why they should camp, even in travelling, where there is no water is a puzzle.'

The going seemed far easier in the afternoon than it had been in the morning, although the conditions were much the same. I had slipped into an unhurried stride, rather like wading through water or stepping slowly and deliberately through a field of tall grass. I found it possible to lean against the wind and by lifting my knees a little higher than usual I could roll one foot over the other without much strain.

The warm wind dried the skin and evaporated perspiration to such an extent that my arms and legs felt slightly cold. I remember thinking that if this was the worst we could expect I had nothing to fear except apprehension. What I didn't know at the time was that the effects of sustained heat and the downpouring of powerful sunlight are slow and insidious and it was possible to go far without realising that much was wrong.

I became very irritable. I had a strong suspicion that Ikky had lost his way and I began to think that he was as much of a rogue as I had been a dupe in accepting his services as a guide, and that we were now in a bigger mess than we should have been if I had not taken him on.

As if he had read my thoughts Ikky suddenly stopped and said something to Mezek. Mezek nodded and turned on me. 'The Turkana,' he said, 'wants to find the *barra barra m'zuri*.' The good road! Feeling thoroughly ill-tempered, I said if he could find any sort of track, good, bad or indifferent, I should be obliged to him. From east to west I could see nothing but lumps of chocolate-coloured lava. It was a landscape for a nightmare and we were unquestionably lost. With irony which was wasted on everyone concerned I asked *how* the Turkana proposed to find the good road.

They told me we should rest a while and while we rested the Turkana would reconnoitre from the top of a hill. I watched him walk away with an easy, open stride, his sandals plopping as he skipped from one piece of sharp-edged rock to another. He seemed to have a lot of confidence; I had very little. Our route lay to the north. The hills were still directly ahead of us, but as far as I could see it was not possible to walk much further across the intervening country. The lava was getting worse and two of the camels flopped down on their bellies as soon as their head-ropes were released. The others stood motionless. A bad sign. Ordinarily they would have wandered off at once to look for food.

Squatting with my back against a rock as hot as a radiator I watched Ikky carefully picking his way towards the higher ground. Possibly I had misjudged him but on long marches I found that irritability invariably rose and fell with the sun. In the early hours of the morning I could make plans, chat to the men, think beautiful thoughts and take a reasonably intelligent interest in what we saw. But after about half-past ten, especially in desolate places or when we'd made an early-morning start, I tended to become morbidly introspective.

This I took to be the 'accidie or white melancholy' described by John Cassian, a fifty-century monk. It seems to be related to 'the destruction that wasteth at noonday . . . a persistent and obnoxious enemy to such as dwell in the desert, disturbing . . . especially about midday, like a fever mounting at a regular time'.

Ikky had by this time shrunk to the size of an ant on grey rock. He scanned the horizon without shading his eyes, looked round once and then walked back as nonchalantly as he had walked away.

As I might have guessed, he told Mezek that the 'good road' was 'not very far'. The camels were dragged to their feet and we marched on. I began to wonder if it was something more than a coincidence that a lake in such a violent landscape had been named after a suicidal prince.

Count Teleki named the lake after his royal master, the Crown Prince Rudolf of Austria, a name wholly unknown to anyone of our company. To the Samburu the Big Water beyond Nyiru is *Basso*; the Turkana know it as *Aman* and the northern tribes as *Gallop*. To me the lake was a will-o'-the-wisp and I began to wonder if we should ever reach it.

Slow as our progress was, it showed that far from justifying my suspicions, Ikky was a thoroughly competent guide. The *barra-barra* he sought was not what I would have called a road. It was a long rib of

Hour before dusk

142

rock that rose from the crusty surface of the lava. Once we got on top of it the going was slithery, but less arduous than the way through the boulders on either side. The rock led to the mouth of a deep gorge, the Sirima, which had nothing to commend it except that at the far end I thought I saw an occasional flicker which might have come from the surface of a large sheet of water.

Before I could ask any questions Ikky indicated that his duties as guide were over. He said that the lake was at the end of the gorge and he was anxious to get back to his own people. He left us, apparently satisfied, with three fish hocks, a length of monofilament line and a few sticks of dried camel meat. When I looked down the gorge again I could not see the flash and Lelean irritated me beyond measure by saying that he knew that *Basso* was not very far.

The wind had sunk to a mere breath, but on the floor of the Sirima it was the hot breath of a boiler-room. It was as if the once molten basalt that towered above us had retained the heat of the volcanoes from which it had been spewed out.

The light flickered again. I wondered at first if it were lightning or the reflection of the sun on distant rocks, but I said nothing to the boys. Lelean I knew would tell me that the lake was not very far away and we should soon be able to prepare a good camp where there was plenty of water. I had heard this many, many times before.

The sun had almost set by the time we came in full view of Rudolf. It was a satin sunset of amber and oyster blue, with the distant hills of Turkanaland painted in bold brushstrokes of purple watercolour. I had thought about the Jade Sea so often that I cannot remember my first impressions except that the lake was olive green and more vast than I had imagined, certainly more beautiful than I could have foreseen. A spiral of birds turned like tea-leaves in the sky. They were wood ibises and pelicans which sank slowly down from a great height, until they became lost in a host of unidentifiable birds on the surface of the water.

A romantic sight. I felt romantic. With a crumbling stucco of dust and sweat on our faces I think we probably looked somewhat romantic and we kept up this appearance until we were within a few hundred yards of the water. Then we acted quite normally.

Karo broke the spell with an exultant yell and started to run down the slope, pulling off his pants on the way. Lelean and Mezek pounded after him, shedding their shirts as they ran. I jumped into the water before I remembered I was wearing a non-waterproof watch. But it was of no great importance. For ten minutes the orderly, reserved relationship between master and men was thrown aside as if it had never existed. We behaved like children.

Karo and Mezek churned up the water in a mock fight while Lelean

Ghostly backwater

stood on his hands on the bottom so that only his wildly thrashing legs were visible. I rolled about in the shallows, floated on my back and duck-dived, head backwards, until I realised that I had drunk a great deal of the water. It tasted and felt as if it were slightly soapy, but despite all I had been told about its soda content it was cool and refreshing and during our days by the lake I never suffered anything more serious than a slight loosening of the bowels.

The camels lumbered up to the water with their lower lips quivering tremulously. They knelt down, extended their snake-like necks and drank and drank until they had to be hauled off into the dusk.

We slept in a crack between two walls of pock-marked lava. Lelean assured me that it was safe to sleep in the open, that is, without the protection of a mosquito net. But I remember very little of that night except that I soon slipped into a satisfying sleep, perhaps the most profound of the whole safari. Whatever the outcome, we had at last reached the Jade Sea.

TALES FROM THE DALES

THEY TELL A tale in Upper Airedale of a sixty-year-old flockmaster on Fountains Fell who, after being engaged for fifteen years, had just married the lady of his choice. As might be imagined the villagers in Malham below that great wall of mountain limestone had much to say. 'Well, there's one thing aboot it,' declared the landlord of the Buck Inn as the last of his customers dutifully filed out for the night, 'if it doesn't turn oot too well, he's noan so long to go-a.'

That story with its stark humour and apparent callousness is fairly typical of a confederation of extremely diverse people with much in common. Before the carvers-up of the old county boundaries got to work without reck or ruth in the early 1970s, Yorkshire was by far the largest of the ancient Shires. With its heavy industries, its mountains and moors, its plains and dales, it is as varied as life itself. It still covers nearly four million acres, almost the size of Wales, and, if you added a half-day's march to its western reaches between Bainbridge and Barkers Fell, it would reach from the Irish Channel to the immense cliffs of the North Sea.

It would follow, therefore, that although a dyed-in-the-wool *Loiner*, a native of Leeds, differs as much from a man of the northern moors as, say, a Clydeside shipwright does from a sheep-gatherer in the Grampians, Yorkshire folk everywhere probably have closer bonds than the Scots. Language devoid of all the silken trimmings of convention is one of them.

I recall a lonely crossroads near the great Cistercian abbey of Rievaulx which at that moment lay almost hidden in a dank mist. There came a noise as of approaching Sherman tanks. A dilapidated combine harvester emerged from the murk. A farmer driving an even older car a little too fast for safety saw it, too late. He braked, skidded and crashed into its side. It sounded like a tram smash.

The two men got out, not even scratched, and surveyed the wreckage. Neither spoke for at least a minute. And then one of them shook his head slowly and said: 'Well ar reckon we could'a done wi'out *that*.'

Taciturnity and conversation are unevenly divided between what I *Malham Tarn*

147

insist on calling the Ridings, the old division of the shire into three parts, from the Norse word *thridjnge*. An importunate stranger may well encounter a degree of bluntness which he is likely to regard as rudeness, especially in the industrial West. They are a sentimental people who tend to disguise innate generosity under a cloak of gruffness. In short, many of them are not immediately easy to get on with.

ROSEDALE

There is a notion that men are like salmon who, however far they voyage in the oceans of the world, are drawn back at last to the streams of their youth. We bought a cottage at Thorgill, on the moors above Rosedale Abbey in Ryedale about ten miles north of Pickering, some years ago. Our first thought was how to handle a mere pocket handkerchief of a garden. The choice seemed obvious. The North Yorks National Park of some 500 square miles is mainly heather-clad. What better than to cultivate a representative selection of heathers so that this old mine-worker's cottage built of brick and sandstone and the moors that surround it on all sides would be in harmony with one another?

The difficulty was that one of the previous owners, Old Charlie, a retired iron miner and an eccentric by anyone's standards, was a dab hand at growing vegetables. Into the plot he dug everything calculated to destroy the extreme acidity of the soil. Unfortunately, with few exceptions, heathers are intolerant of lime and it took many loads of local peat to neutralise what he had buried, which included two of his ceilings that fell down and a great deal of ancient mortar from his outside lavatory.

However, within five years we managed to establish complete ground cover of little heatherlings and then began the task of ensuring that groups of mature plants were in flower all the year round. This is not difficult.

Eight different kinds of heather grow wild in Britain and Ireland. A few are rare. Three are common and all three – the ubiquitous ling, the cross-leaved heath and the wine-coloured bell heather – flourish within 200 yards of our plot. It is from these eight different kinds of wild heathers, plus a few other southern European species which are at their best when native plants are cowering under wind winds, that nurserymen have built up stocks of many hundreds of cultivars and variants.

We take some modest pride in our plot because the rarer cultivars are so hardy that, occasionally, we can supply a large nursery down in

Thorgill in winter

the Vale of Pickering when their own stocks are nipped by frost. And in turn we can dip freely into their sophisticated beds for whatever we want.

Ling, the commonest species of all, has been used for thousands of years by highlanders and moorland dwellers who, out of sheer necessity, were obliged to use heather for grazing, building material, beds, brooms and even drinks. There used to be a famous brew of heather ale, much praised by the Celtic bards, but the recipe seems to have been lost long before Julius Caesar turned up with his fighting men dressed in tin and flannel.

Today, heather in its youthful stages is an important source of food for errant sheep and the grouse at which the rich blast away regardless of cost, a highly profitable exercise for the local lords of the moors. When huge expanses of ling reach a certain height, usually after about ten or fifteen years, the plants become bushy and have to be burnt down

Garden in March

After the burn

in patches by keepers who strive to control the fires. They are not always successful. If an unexpected wind springs up, the blaze can reach furnace temperatures of 800 °C and more, whereupon not only the straggly plants but the peat below, which harbours the minute but long-lasting seeds of heather, may be destroyed. This is such a serious matter that laws governing the burn have been laid down but rarely enforced since the fifteenth century.

We have grown accustomed to seeing those ominous clouds of smoke on the skyline and hope only that it doesn't affect incoming bird life intent on nesting – golden plover and the like, which are far more important to us than cackling grouse.

An unrelieved expanse of heather is an artefact. It is the produce of burning. The first botanical colonists on the bare humus among the whitened stalks are minute algae, lichens and mosses including an intricate genus *Polytrichum*, the hair moss. Then, perhaps, we may see the bright green shoots of fruitful bilberry until at last, with a degree of luck, may appear a sprout of heather like a defiant flag on an almost overtaken battlefield. I say with luck because the enemy is always there, the invasive bracken, ready to take over any open ground.

Sarkless Kitty

The curtain rose on drama in the tempestuous year of 1787 when, after months of snow, the river Dove flooded the lower end of Farndale. To reach the nearest villages of Gillamoor and Hutton-le-Hole, the local folk were obliged to ford the Dove at what is now the Lowna Bridge, and then could only do so on the back of a reliable horse. To show that he had become a man, young Willie Dixon of Hutton twice waded across but, as most people knew, it was only to impress Kitty Garthwaite, and was unnecessary, too, since she had decided the previous year who should become Mrs Willie Dixon. But she had had doubts. There were rumours that Willie had been with other lasses at times when only those courting seriously should be seen together after dusk.

In April of that year Kitty began to be concerned that their wedding should not be long delayed. There was more than one reason. But although they met together regularly at Lowna on his side of the river, so that he could carry her over to the Gillamoor road, the rumours about Willie's infidelity began to centre on that girl at Castleton who would inherit considerable property.

Kitty pressed him. He refused to give straight answers. On Whit *When spring comes* Sunday evening in May they quarrelled. Angry words were said on

both sides. Willie left Kitty there by the alder tree in the dark. Nobody saw her alive again. What had happened to the distracted girl could be easily reconstructed from moist footprints and clothing scattered about in different fields. When they fished her body out from the pool below the ford she was wearing only her white sark, a sort of chemise.

The tragedy divided the villages. There were not a few who said that, since it was clearly a case of suicide, she should be buried at the cross-roads with, if the thing had to be done properly, a stake through her left breast. Her mother, widowed only a few months earlier, could scarcely speak. She would not leave her cottage. At last she told the vicar that as by rights her daughter was already Mrs Dixon, it was Willie who should have to attend to the burying. But nobody had seen Willie since the previous afternoon.

Monday passed. And Tuesday. The unclaimed body was laid on a pile of hay at the Old Mill where a charitable soul, a Mrs Agar, after doing the last offices, removed the poor girl's sark and washed it, covering her meanwhile with some fresh sacking.

During a furious storm of rain on the Wednesday morning Willie arrived home utterly distracted. It seems that without telling anyone what he was up to he had ridden to York at dawn on Monday, hoping to bring back a special wedding licence that day. He had overlooked the fact that it was Whit Monday and the offices were closed. He spent a frustrating Tuesday finding witnesses and persuading a reluctant magistrate to give him a licence. He then galloped back.

At Helmsley, twelve miles away, they told him what had happened. He made straight away for the Old Mill where Mrs Agar did her best to comfort him before she took him down to the barn. He brushed past her, ran up the steps and then turned round to look at the old lady, astonished. The barn was empty. The imprint on the hay was clear enough, the sacks lay neatly folded, but the body itself and the clean sark were gone.

Mrs Agar was more surprised than he was – she had seen the body the previous night. But Willie, thinking that the girl's mother had somehow arranged matters, hastened to her cottage. She could tell him nothing. Nor could anyone else. Recalling that Kitty had a distant relative at the head of the dale, a half-cousin who was very fond of her, he rode there, but could learn no more. She, like everybody else, thought the body lay in the barn.

All that long day Willie, who by then was almost exhausted, rode the length of Farndale and Rosedale until, late at night, he knocked on the door at the vicarage at Lastingham, only to discover that once again he was the first to bring the news. But it was far from being the end of the matter. The next morning they found his horse quietly grazing on the east bank of the river near Lowna ford, and Willie's body was recovered

from the same pool from which, four days earlier, they had recovered the blanched corpse of Kitty Garthwaite.

If the majority of the villagers thought that, like his mistress, he had taken his own life, they admitted that there was at least the possibility that his tired horse might have stumbled and thrown him into the swollen river, and he was given a good Christian burial.

Three weeks later two young boys came home at dusk with a strange tale. They had seen Kitty sitting by the ford but, as one of them put it, 'she had nowt on'. She smiled at them and waved her sark. They were sent to bed early for making up such a daft tale.

In the autumn of that year the riderless horse of the second of a series of victims cantered up the hill to the village just before the pub closed. It was recognised as belonging to a traveller who, against advice, had said he intended to ford the river that night. The next morning they found his body in what became known as Sarkless Kitty's pool.

The apparition appeared to others who were more fortunate. Local folk, always men, saw her at night, sometimes sitting in her tree beckoning, at other times running along the bank or wading in the water, naked, holding up her sark. It was said that animals, particularly horses turned out to graze, would not go near the ford after sundown. But *Lowna beck* strangers were lured into that deep pool; and when over the years ten or more were drowned there the villagers approached the vicar of Lastingham to see whether with bell, book and candle he could exorcise the unquiet spirit in the name of the Blessed St Cedd. He confessed he didn't much like the idea. It smelt of superstition. But at last he agreed.

The service was the traditional Order for the Burial of the Dead, except that the priest stood in the shallows of the pool and after the words 'dust to dust' he added 'water to water'. It was reported that Kitty 'did not trouble the company with her visible presence and the gathering quietly and reverently dispersed'.

Until the late Richard Crosland, one of the founders of the Folk Museum at Hutton-le-Hole, came across the Armadale Bible, Kitty was largely forgotten. Reports of the reappearance of the ghost were, to say the least, tenuous, but the sequel is more remarkable by far than the events which provoked it.

Among some books at a local sale Mr Crosland bought an old leather-bound large-print Bible for a few shillings. It was inscribed *Joseph Armadale from his parents 25.5th m. 1765*. Quite by chance he noticed a small 'x' against Matthew 27, verse 60, and at the foot of the page *x – inside back*. A closer inspection showed that something had been inserted between the endpapers and the board. It was a large sheet of paper, folded and covered with small neat handwriting, and signed simply *H. A.*

Henry, the only surviving son of Joseph and Eliza Armadale of Rudland, the ridge above Farndale, disclosed that his younger sister Mary had died and was buried in the 'Quakers' garth', a walled enclosure about half a mile above the present Lowna Bridge. They buried her on the Friday before Whit Sunday, 1787 – three days before Kitty's body was recovered.

On the Tuesday night, when the suicide was being discussed by almost everyone in the neighbourhood, young Henry and his mother and father, good Quakers all, sat around the table of their cottage 'up Rudland', heavy with their private grief. Precisely how the conversation went must be in part inferred from events which Henry felt should be set down clearly for the sake of his conscience. I shall relate it largely in Crosland's words.

They said grace. They ate their meal. As usual his father read a portion of the Gospels. It happened to be the chapter in which Joseph of Arimathea went to Pilate and begged the body of Jesus. Mr Armadale's voice paused as he came to the words: 'He wrapped it in a clean linen cloth. And laid it in his new tomb which he had hewn out in the rock, and he rolled a great stone to the door of the sepulchre, and departed.'

After a short silence they all retired but, as he understood it, neither father nor mother could sleep. She said, 'That poor child under the sacks is on me mind.'

A pause, and then his father asked, 'Eliza, dost thou think Joseph left the bodies of those two thieves hanging?'

'Nay, I think he must have covered them somewhere.'

Another pause and then: 'His own new tomb, Eliza?'

The only answer was a woman trying to control her sobs.

Then Joseph said, 'Dost thou think this is a leading?'

'There can be no doubt about it.'

Joseph got out of bed saying, 'Then there can be no delay. It must be done at once.'

'I will accompany thee,' she said.

They rose together and dressed, and whilst Eliza stopped to take something from a drawer, Joseph brought round the old mare laden with pack-saddle, ropes, a spade and a pick.

Avoiding the few houses on the way, they crossed into Farndale and down to the Old Mill where Kitty lay. The barn was not fastened, and at a sign from Eliza, Joseph stood aside while she went in with her bundle. When he entered a few minutes later the body was wrapped in a clean linen sheet, and as he lifted it to carry it out a fragrance of sweet herbs surrounded him. The burden was quickly transferred to the mare, which had quietly waited and had made no noise at all, and they again took the track, this time for the burying garth.

On their arrival Eliza sat a while with the body, Joseph going in with his tools. She could hear that he was at work, but there was no sound of the pick, which surprised her. She was more surprised when she entered the garth to see her husband hard at work, opening the very grave in which their only daughter had been laid less than five days earlier.

Joseph saw her coming and, before she had recovered from her surprise, whispered, 'It could be nowhere else, my dear. Her own new tomb.' So there, close above the coffin of their daughter, carefully bedded in dry leaves so that the earth and stones should not lie too heavily upon her, they buried Kitty Garthwaite.

The Lyke Wake

Silpho Moor stands a little to the south east of Whisperdale, a tributary of the Derwent. Today it's a rather lonely, nobody-about sort of place because visibility is limited on the edge of those dreary manmade forests not far inland from Scarborough. But let us go back to that fearful winter of 1809 when the Iron Duke defeated the French at Talavera and Napoleon, somewhat discomforted by it all, decided to divorce Josephine.

For nearly four months Silpho had been under a blanket of snow in places as high as Job Wainwright's barn door, a big barn since he and his three lads made those thick-wheeled carts on which you could carry almost anything. Job knew they were in for a proper mauling when late at night he heard the gabblerack, the trumpeting of wild geese flying south nearly a month before their accustomed time. And so he made plans. Six sheep were pole-axed and dressed soon after the long nights set in.

As for Granny, he had a shrewd idea she hadn't long to go as soon as he heard the gabble on three successive nights. He had made a coffin for her the previous year, but she'd got better. No matter. It was a good piece of elm cut with care. As she lovingly fingered the lightly polished wood, Granny said she could trust her favourite grandson to do her right. She died soon afterwards.

So it came about that they half packed that stout oblong box with ice and lowered her into it, gently, on the eve of All Saints' tide. There, in a drift at the back of the barn, she lay for over a hundred days with the lid propped up with two bricks. Better to let the frozen air in. And who knew? Some neighbours might want a last look.

And now it were thawing, proper. Everything dripped. The Derwent began to foam with snow-melt. Job knew she ought to have been dirged to the old church at Hackness the week before. But he wanted to help where he could. Just before the first of three appalling storms isolated the moors around what is today Broxa Forest, Death had come to some important decisions.

Alf Spenthorpe at Swarth Howe lost his only lad. His neighbour under Barnes Cliff had fared worse. His missus and a suckling died within a week. There were three waiting for interment at Thieves Dike and two in Troutsdale: epidemic pneumonia. Nine bodies in need of shriving were frozen within a radius of three miles.

Not long after the March hiring they set out for Hackness in dismal column with Father Roberts, an open-minded man, ahead of the procession. Job, the wisest, certainly the richest local man, led the Dirgers. Four children carried the pathetically small box that contained the earthly remains of the little one. To the accompaniment of Charlie with his trombone the Dirgers sang:

> *Fra' Whinny Moor when thoo art passed,*
> *Iverry neet an' all*
> *'Till Brig o' Dread thoo cums at Last,*
> *An' Christ tak oop thi saul.*

Silpho Moor   The custom is of unknown origin, the meaning almost wholly lost in

the Yorkshire of the fourteenth or fifteenth centuries. Perhaps only those who have crossed Wheeldale or the Fylingdales Moors with storm and darkness threatening can get a glimmer of what it betokens. The belief is that tracks where unhallowed bodies have been carried sanctify and render that last gangway unfit for any other purpose except passage of the dead.

Keeping It in the Family

On those high moors that stand above Ryedale you may hear a strange tale of a man who lost almost everything he valued except a cat with one black ear, but I shall say no more except in broad terms since he lived with his sister, happily, as man and wife, a practice not uncommon in the country. It came about, as it often does, through the death of a member of two closely related families.

Tom and his cousin Herbert, as I shall call them, got on well. They were alike in many ways. They had gone to school together. They used each other's gear. They farmed adjacent land. They didn't bother overmuch about common boundaries, and when Herbert married Tom's sister she kept an eye on her brother's house as well, suggesting little improvements here and there in the way that only a woman can.

When war broke out, Tom, the single man, promptly volunteered for the army, knowing the farm would be left in good hands, but they turned him down on the grounds of some minor heart disorder he knew nothing about. So Herbert went off, and Herbert died in France within a year.

Tom grieved as deeply as his sister, perhaps more so because for a long time he acted as though Herbert would soon be back on the farm and when, eventually, he took to drink in a big way, it took all her powers of persuasion to get him to cut it down and go out occasionally at night. But with the three-fold cord of love, including that subtle one of someone who reminds you of someone else, she persevered and in time it would have been difficult to find a closer, more affectionate pair.

Many years passed. Tom built up a fine flock of sheep. At the sales they knew him for a dead-straight dealer and, as for that sister of his, they reckoned her a good lass, always ready to give a hand to the needful.

Nobody knows what Tom did shortly after she died. It was all so unexpected, but within a year he had sold both holdings, keeping only the small cottage in which he lived. From time to time a van came up from the stores with groceries and liquor. The one friend he saw very occasionally recalls seeing him sitting on the porch, stroking his beloved cat, all that remained of his household.

A curious creature. Like her mother who had been Herbert's cat before his cousin married, she had a fine creamy-white coat relieved only by one black ear. A farmer's cat. She liked to be stroked, to be fed. But she knew her way around and at night she roamed. Kittens came, and in country fashion, the kittens went straight into the rain tub. The cat's only reaction was that when her belly began to swell noticeably, she wasn't to be seen around for a time.

One day Tom collapsed. He fell down in the kitchen, unable even to lift his head, and the chances are that if the van driver hadn't turned up that afternoon and literally dragged him out of the house, he would have died. At the hospital he remained in a state of partial coma for several days. It seems that the old heart trouble had reasserted itself. Yet they assured him it wasn't really serious if he took things easy for a few months. But Tom said he was going to die, and summoned his old friend.

'If you go back to the farm and kill the old cat,' he said, 'you can take the chickens. There isn't much else, and I shan't be leaving this place except when they carry me out.' But Tom didn't die. He went back to a farm more deserted than ever. No sister. No cat and no chickens. He talked vaguely about getting a dog, but for the most part he sat and drank and stared out to the open moor, to the great waste beyond his patch of garden.

And then one evening, just before dusk, he caught a glimpse of the cat with one black ear. He could scarcely believe his eyes. He jumped to his feet; he called, but it ran away quickly. Indignantly he went straight round to see his friend. What sort of trick was this? Had he

Sherriff's pit

killed the animal or not? His friend assured him that the cat had not only been killed but buried that very same day. He could show him the spot.

About the same time the next evening the animal reappeared. It seemed extremely timid. But by placing a saucer of milk nearer and nearer to the house each day Tom gradually enticed the animal indoors and picked it up. As he stroked the creature lovingly, he felt the testicles of a young tom cat. Tired of losing her offspring, the mother had raised a litter in the woods and one of her sons had returned home.

CHAMPIONS OF THE MINES

Around the bar were Ned Micklethwaite, a rose-grower from Eskdale; Arthur Champion, an old engineer who helped to dismantle the mine above Thorgill; and John, the flockmaster from the other side of the valley. The talk ranged from sheep-gathering to life in the dales as Ned and Arthur remembered it, when over 1,000 miners were hired to dig for iron ore at the rate of a shilling a ton. Since the mines closed the total population has fallen to less than two hundred.

The subject arose from a casual remark of mine about some work done on the cottage by George Wetherill, reckoned to be one of the best stone-masons for miles around. Ned put me in touch with him. George, he said, could judge a piece of good freestone with his eyes closed, listening to the ring of the chisel. The master mason cut into those honey-coloured slabs slowly and rhythmically, pausing only to run his fingers over the exposed skin, gently, as lovers do. As he used to quarry much of the stone he dressed, I took up his invitation to watch him at work in his own yard. On hearing this, Arthur suggested I might drop into his place and 'have a look at t' owd buzzer'.

In the old days the buzzer or siren, a huge brass affair, governed the life of the dale. From dawn to sundown it wailed at regular intervals, summoning the miners to Sheriff's Pit, now a gaunt ruin on the track above Thorgill. When they closed the pit down, Arthur, the old engineer, took the buzzer home to Castleton, a few miles to the north where his son now runs a three star garage.

All three men knew a great deal about the days when they built the old Reading Room and danced to that curious jingle about King Henry, but there are conventions to be observed among local folk. If a new-comer asks too many questions in a pub in the West Riding, he is apt to be shot down hard by a blunt remark from those who pride them-selves on their bluntness, but up here on these north-eastern moors they are more polite and sometimes, you may think, more devious. They

imply rather than say where you stand in their opinion. Yet this is a *Farndale* generalisation. Arthur, I felt, would have been prepared to talk about the mines until closing time. Ned had his reservations. Hard to explain to an outsider, he said.

Why? I asked. John thought that to strangers most of us play the part we are expected to play. 'When them seventy quid a week steel-workers from Teesside come down here in their flashy cars, looking the place over, they look on me as just another bloody yokel,' he said.

Most of our locals will talk to you alone, but until they know what you are up to, they haven't much to say in each other's company. Rising to go, John and Arthur both suggested I might care to look in and see them if I ever walked their way. They said goodnight, leaving me to make what I could of Ned.

Silence for about as long as it took us to sink another bottle of New-castle Brown, then, with some hesitation, he began to talk about the feasts held when they celebrated the anniversary of the Wesleyan Chapel. They laid the food out on trestle-tables in a freshly lime-washed wagon shed. But it wasn't the thought of home-cured ham, the rounds of beef, the bread and the salty yellow butter that stirred his memory. The walls were covered with sheets and on those sheets the womenfolk pinned hundreds of roses; sweet-scented briars, pink and white fresh from the hedgerow, and the scarlet ramblers and the old Damask and Bourbons from the minister's garden. 'I can still smell 'em,' he said. 'It were like a loft full of ripe apples.'

I wondered how he would fare in places where the air is acrid from exhaust fumes. Wouldn't get him into a city for all the tea in China, he said. For as long as he could remember he had lived in a world scented from season to season as plainly as changes in the temperature.

'What about January?' I asked.

'Depends where you are,' he said. 'Bracken on t'moors is getting a bit mouldy, but you can sniff the larch sprouts in the forest. Not much growing wild, though there's generally some winter heliotrope by the roadside. It starts to flower in December and smells of almonds.'

Snowdrops put him in mind of honey, especially if you kept a bowlful in a warm room. In his opinion there wasn't much to distinguish the spring earthy smell of primroses from wild daffodils, and as for violets, what else did they smell of but violets? Or at least those that *had* a smell. 'Most don't smell of owt much,' he said. Cowslips had the whiff of aniseed and hawthorns in bloom were foul, he thought. Like stinking fish. Nearly as bad as cuckoo-pints or wild arums. But from June onwards the air became scented everywhere, and most of all he loved his roses and wallflowers and fresh-cut hay.

To all this I listened, intrigued and a little saddened, for although I can well recall the aroma of bluebell woods, wild thyme crushed underfoot on the Downs and night-scented stock and honeysuckle in gardens at dusk, my ability to detect a wild range of smells has all but disappeared. Curiously enough my sense of taste is fairly acute, but for the rest I'm obliged to rely largely on my eyes and ears and other sensory faculties less easy to describe, such as the differing spring of the ground underfoot, the feel of the sun and the wind. And rain, too, though in moderation.

Ned knew a lot about local place names and satisfied my curiosity about Hob Crag which overlooks the road as we approach the cottage. That word hob, so common in place names hereabouts, is a variant of hobgoblin or sprite. Hob has a homely ring about it. It cuts the little devils down to size. Hobs used to make a nuisance of themselves in various ways, curdling the milk, tripping up granddad, pinching the maids in their beds, leaving the impression that the master fancied them. An old miner who swore he didn't believe in them fell over the edge of that gaunt crag one night, and innumerable tales are told of what went on at Hob Farm at the foot of the escarpment.

On the other side of the crag lies Farndale, a dale renowned for richer pastures and little wild daffodils. The tale there is of a farmer who, after putting up with a particularly malevolent hob for years, decided to flit,

*Below the King
Henry*

Road to the mines

that is, to pull out and try his luck elsewhere. In an effort to get away quietly, he loaded up his most prized possessions at dawn, intending to come back for the rest later.

To his discomfiture, as he drove off, a neighbour seeing him said, 'Is thou *really* flittin', George?' And before he could reply a voice from somewhere among the piled-up gear replied, 'Aye, we'se flittin'.' At which the farmer, concluding sadly that no change of abode could be of any help, turned his horse's head homewards.

Yet if in certain places there were troublesome things to be contended with, in others nearby the youngsters met for sport and love, and in one, under Gill Crag, for both. This is the crag we can see from our kitchen window. Below it lies an old Methodist chapel and the village courtship ground. If the ministers knew what went on after dark on a certain date, their opinions have long since been forgotten. But old men say that both they and their fathers made it there for the first time.

One hinted at a fair amount of belly-bumping 'under t'crag' from Eastertide onwards, but he, like the others, spoke of the place with quiet affection. During what seems to have been a kissing game enacted on the evening of the chapel anniversary, the young lads and lasses of the village formed circles and slowly paraded round each other, singing or reciting some verses about the exploits of King Henry. Could Ned recall them? He said it went something like:

> *King Henry was King Henry's son*
> *And now the royal race is done*
> *So choose the one that you love best, and . . .*

And choose they did. The couples paired off. They wandered up to the foot of the crag, where, in the evening light, vows were exchanged and often consummated. Old folk he knew were 'sort of married at a King Henry'.

But why King Henry? Because of his habit of swopping one wife for another? Because he united the Houses of York and Lancaster? Nobody seemed to know. But Ned thought the words were written down in some book he had and said he would try to find it.

The next day, a very superior sort of day with clouds like little puffs of cannon smoke, I phoned Arthur Champion, suggesting that, if he could get the buzzer working, perhaps I could walk over and have a word with him. Rumbling with amusement, he said he wouldn't mind giving the thing a whirl if the mechanics weren't using the compressed-air cylinders, but first he'd have to tell the police and the fire brigade – 'Otherwise folk might think another ruddy war had broken out.' I said I'd be with him the next morning.

With his flat cloth cap pulled down hard over his ears, there was something about the thickset posture and manner of Arthur Champion that put you in mind of an amiable bear. He didn't often speak until he was spoken to but, with his confidence gained, he carried on telling stories nicely punctuated with shoulder-shaking chuckles. He had spent his early years in Thorgill helping dismantle Sheriff Pit, where his father had been the chief foundryman and his grandfather, Old Harry, the manager.

Old Harry, he said, had done a lot in his time. Among much else he made both a violin and the frame of a piano out of some old seasoned pit boards. 'Aye,' Arthur went on, 'an' atop of all that 'ee 'ad twenty-one kids twice.' At my look of incredulity he nodded gravely and produced a faded photograph of the family, including Granny Esther in a black straw hat decorated with forget-me-nots. He explained that the twenty-first child died, 'so that when next 'un came along she'd had twenty-one twice', a joke which I suspect he'd told many times before. He looked down at the old lady in the decorated straw hat and shook his head. 'Don't think she ever 'ad time to put it on,' he said.

During our talk it came out that, by curious coincidence, Arthur had taken his bride to what is now our cottage. That was sixty years ago. He and his son Derrick now run the garage at Castleton, a big place with welding shops and hydraulic lifts. A far cry from his first wage of fourpence a day at Thorgill.

While mechanics attached cylinders of compressed air to the buzzer, Arthur sat back and talked about the poverty-stricken life of the miners in the days of the Good Queen. He remembered them well. Perhaps too well. Miners in isolated parts of the dale thought nothing of delivering their wives' babies, and in the absence of their menfolk some women occasionally delivered their own. Nobody took a holiday, year in and year out. Wouldn't be a job waiting for them if they did. Hard enough to hold down what they'd got. The buzzer blew at six o'clock in the morning. By that time the miners had to be right inside the galleries, ready for work. For some who had to walk several miles this meant getting up at half-past four in the morning or earlier. For breakfast, or what Arthur called 'a bit o' bait', the buzzer blew at eight o'clock when most of the miners squatted down on their heels and ate bread and jam. It blew again at twelve for their midday meal and once more when they trudged home after an eleven-hour day.

To bring in some overtime money, Arthur undertook breakdown jobs that had to be carried out when the mines closed down at the weekends. He set off for work early on Saturday morning, sleeping at the pit, and walked back on Monday night. For several months he never saw his first child awake. It lay sleeping when he left the cottage in the morning and had been put to bed before he returned home.

In the feeble light of their lamps deep underground the miners saw

*Champions of the
mines*

the green eyes of rats, eager to snatch any morsel left uncovered; they heard the supporting timber groaning, or 'talking' as they called it; and they were often wet through from the seepage above. To aerate that labyrinth of galleries, the management kept fires burning at the foot of the deepest shaft, a contrivance that sucked in air from the drifts in the hillside below, but the air often became so foul that their candles flickered out and men staggered to the entrance, panting for breath.

For putting up with that sort of life the miners received about a shilling a ton for what they dug out. It might have been one and threepence for high-grade ore, but it usually amounted to no more than six or seven shillings a day, and for that pittance they had to do all their own drilling and blasting with black powder bought expensively from the management. If the charge blew back without shattering the rock, they might be out of pocket on a day's work. But they burrowed like moles, saving time between shots by biting off an inch or two from their fuses, thereby risking a premature explosion in their efforts to dig out more of the rusty red rock.

Arthur decided to look elsewhere. For a few pounds he bought an old car, a two-cylinder Wolseley with steps for getting in at the back. He said he couldn't afford any tyres but by stuffing the tubes with grass he got the thing going and eventually did some taxi work. With help with his father he forged all his own tools; he developed a passion for rebuilding car engines: Albions, Napiers, T-model Fords and Chryslers. He brought out an old photograph of one he tinkered with for years, a collector's piece, a belt-driven one-cylinder Marshall with solid iron wheels, made in 1896. In bottom gear it rattled along at three miles an hour and made scarcely more than twice that speed in top. To stop it running backwards on steep hills he equipped it with a novel sort of brake, a spike under the chassis that could be driven into the road. He bought the car for twelve quid as scrap, and sold it years later for £450. Who knows what it might be worth today?

He retained his life-absorbing passion for mechanical objects: not the passion of a collector, but that of a craftsman working with the precision of a clockmaker. Although he later drove an almost silent Mercedes and lived in a fine villa above Castleton, he constantly used a lathe or a gear-cutting machine, inventing devices which were patented, such as a shot-firing device for ICI, but for his own pleasure forever making things out of steel, copper or brass.

'Buzzer's ready,' he said. 'I tell you it don't half hum.' The understatement of the year. He pressed a switch and from that long out-of-work awakener came a groan that arose to an ear-piercing wail, at close quarters a fearful noise. I waved my hands. I couldn't stand it a moment longer, but assured him it sounded fine. As he seemed a little disappointed I didn't want to hear it a second time – at least not in a shed with a galvanised iron roof – I suggested he turned it on half an hour later as I neared the top of the dale on foot. And from a distance of about two miles I heard the old summoner as thousands of miners must have heard it; more melodic in the open air, but ominous in its insistence.

Winter signpost,
Ralph's Cross

171

Telouet: Kasbah of the King-Makers

APART FROM THAT never-to-be-forgotten memory of Man Friday's footprints in the sand, few literary sights or sounds were more stirring to an adolescent of my generation that P. C. Wren's compelling clichés about the adventures of Beau Geste and his companions in the Foreign Legion 'amid veritable oceans of sand'. In later years I spent some time with Gavin Maxwell who had just written *Lords of the Atlas*. He suggested I should travel among people who really understood camels, the haughty Tuareg, 'The Forgotten of God'. Much the same was said by Général Augustine Guillaume, the former Governor General of Morocco who entertained me on my walk through Europe. He called those arid wastes 'nests of intrigue' and implied the French did almost nothing to improve their lot.

Time we went there, so my wife and I – for once not a traveller on my own – booked a ticket to Morocco.

We quickly found that the exotic, the almost medieval quality of Marrakesh defied even the hyperbole of the tourists' guide sheets. When the westering sun seems to splash the Moorish stonework with blood, the Dj'mma El F'naa, the largest and liveliest square in the place, throbs with the sound of goatskin drums and the twang of something that resembles a zither. There are sinuous dancers from the Berber tribe of Blue People whose skins are stained with indigo from their traditional clothing. Bare-footed acrobats turn double somersaults in mid-air.

Snake charmers squat in front of detoxified cobras. Here are storytellers, mime artists, fire-eaters, swiggers down of boiling water and shoals of beggars, from toddlers to toothless. Here you can buy junk or superb stuff and hire almost anything from a rickety *calèche* to a beautiful Berber boy. Dense circles of spectators of various colours exude a variety of smells: mint tea, sweat, crushed oranges, saffron, coffee, fresh donkey dung and local pot known as *kif*.

The Dj'mma El F'naa is a mishmash of merchandise and merriment, *Haughty Tuareg*

173

Circles of spectators

Westering sun

Moroccan musician

Local dancers

Charming snakes

Local news

yet the name is Arabic for 'the gathering ground of the dead'. It dates from the days when undemocratic sultans and pashas displayed the severed heads of those who displeased them on a palisade of spikes. These hideous warnings were pickled in brine to prolong their shelf life. The Dj'mma symbolises the tortuous history that Morocco underwent for 2,000 years before she gained her independence. Marrakesh stands on the fertile plain of Haouz, ringed by the high peaks of the Atlas. The horizon resembles a mirage – remote, forbidding, snow-covered for much of the year. That's where we were heading.

The problem was to find a reliable guide. Hotel guides are not allowed to take on private commissions and neither the arrogant French nor the government agencies are prepared even now to say much about their quislings, especially the Glaoui brothers, Madani and T'hami. As for their *kasbah* or stronghold, Telouet, 'the place that reeks of blood', it lay right off the road, they said. It was difficult to get there. The ruins were dangerous though in time they might be restored. Eventually we were obliged to settle in kind – English books and cassettes in return for transportation and interpretation – for the services of a splendid young fellow know as Zouhir the Scholar, a man with the air of a seminarist in his jet-black *djellebah*. With his hand on his heart, he said he could borrow the great silver key of the huge door of the *kasbah*. He also knew a great deal about *glaouise*, which has come to mean betrayed.

We failed to reach the *kasbah* on two occasions. White, impenetrable cloud enveloped the formidable Tiz-n-Tishka at a height of 6,000 feet, halfway to Quartzazarte on the fringe of the Sahara and some 150 miles to the south east of Marrakesh. We sat in the Land-rover for what seemed like hours amid that most formidable sound – silence, broken only by the occasional wail of jackals. On the third run we got through that ever-mounting serpentine road fringed by eucalyptus trees. One incident alone punctuated the journey. Near Ait Barka, halfway up the pass, we heard a fusillade of gun shots. A local rebellion? Zouhir grinned and pulled into a grove of date palms. Below a long embankment of cactus bushes about twenty finely got-up horsemen were galloping flat out and firing long-barrelled muzzle-loaders as they rode – a re-enactment of a *harka*, a raiding party. *Harka* literally means 'a burning'. They were getting ready for their Independence Day celebrations, a grim reminder of how their forebears lived in the *bled el siba*, southern Morocco, the Land beyond the Law.

We topped the pass in a gale of polar-cold wind, threw away a couple of thousand feet and swung east down a small macadamised road which degenerated into a mule track. Through field glasses, I could just make out a huge fortress of brick and sun-baked mud far ahead. At last, Telouet, the *kasbah* of the king-makers. Before we mounted a steep, boulder-strewn defile, an old man leading a donkey gave Zouhir the local news. Impatient as I was to get to the fortress, it was intriguing to hear that his neighbour Ben Bachir, 'the father of the snakes', had been having a profitable week with his forked stick. Yet another detour took us into a Berber village where a curly-headed fellow with silver teeth showed us hooded cobras and rock vipers in baskets. He waggled one five-footer – still undoctored, he claimed – uncomfortably close to my nose for six dirhams (about fifty pence). They were on sale to the snake-charmers of Marrakesh.

The dilapidated *kasbah* are towers of tragedy that leave no room for regret. As Mohammed V, father of the present King Hassan, put it: 'A monument to death and tyranny, immense, irregular, vulgar in its violence, it leaps to view behind a ramshackle village.' Zouhir waved to it with a dramatic gesture and then shrugged his shoulders. After a word with the ancient guardian who lingers on to tend the relic of an extinct dynasty, our friend and interpreter put the huge silver key into my hand.

Behind the double doors are ruins of exquisitely tiled reception chambers, banqueting rooms, harems for wives and concubines and, deep below, the layered dungeons from which few heavily shackled prisoners ever emerged alive. Several blocks had collapsed, others were shored up with wooden buttresses riddled with dry rot. Pointing through holes in dry outer walls as we scrambled from floor to floor on ledges and piles of rubbish, Zouhir recounted more of its history, giving dramatic emphasis to all I'd heard from Gavin Maxwell.

'There are the old salt mines,' he said. We saw the crest of a long ridge that glistened in the sun. 'And that's one of the very old caravan trails,' he added, pointing to a scribble of a track through the breasts of the distant mountains.

Before their meteoric rise to power at the beginning of this century, the Glaoui brothers – who weren't particularly well off to start with – inherited what eventually proved to be an immense salt mine. Traders came from as far away as Mauretania and Senegal to swap ivory and captive black women for camel trains and salt. But Allah had far greater things in store for them. In the terrible winter of 1893, the reigning Sultan, Moulay Hassan, returned from a disastrous expedition to the Land beyond the Law, a grievously sick man in the train of a hungry and fever-beset army.

Madani, the older brother, foresaw a golden opportunity. To attack, rout and loot the feeble forces of Moulay in the mountains would bring against him all the ambitious *caids* of the south. If, on the other hand, the Sultan became indebted to him through help under the sacred oath of brotherhood, Madani could rely on the powerful chieftains of the rich lands to the north. Madani staked almost everything he could raise on lavish hospitality, guards of honour and mendacious hints that he could summon up 10,000 rifles.

Distant Atlas

Towers of tragedy

Harka

Tishka Pass

The silver key

Sole harem window

The feasting and entertainment for the almost prostrate king went on for days and when at last he departed for the nearest city, Marrakesh, Moulay gave Madani jewels and made him his personal *khalifa*, his representative in the Lawless Country. More important, he gave him ammunition and weaponry, including a 77 mm bronze Krupp cannon, the only piece of heavy mobile artillery outside the imperial Chereefian Army.

Thereafter events moved quickly. The Sultan died. His heir, a young weakling with an opportunistic chamberlain, succeeded him. Rebellion spread throughout the land. Under the guise of peace-keepers, the French moved in with highly mobile forces, the native *harkas*, the equivalent of commandos. Madani waited until he could be certain who commanded the best armies and joined them, stealthily at first and then under a formal treaty with France. *Glaouise* was at work. Morocco underwent a turbulent forty years under a succession of French commanders. First Madani and then at his death his brother T'hami became the richest and most powerful *caids* in Morocco.

T'hami, a shrewd man of eloquence and charm, levied a tax on all the teeming whores of Marrakesh. He acquired a near-monopoly on the sale of *kif*, olives, almonds, saffron, dates and mint. His annual revenue from one huge grove of olives at Agadal was underestimated at thirty million francs.

His ostentation, his delight in a fleet of luxurious but thoughtfully armoured limousines, was matched but not exceeded by his inherent capacity for ruthlessness and cruelty. Powerful adversaries were secretly kidnapped, subjected to fearful torture in the dungeons of Telouet for useful information about who was doing what, and then methodically flayed to death. One was thrown into a pit of hungry lions where one beast took a sizeable bite out of the side of his face while the others worked on him from the feet upwards. T'hami had powerful friends in Paris and London, including Winston Churchill, who invited him to the Coronation in 1953. As one sworn enemy of the clan put it: 'Between them there existed the mutual respect and sympathy of brigands.'

But the brothers and their hordes of dependent children, black, white and khaki, probably around sixty or seventy in all, had underestimated the growth and strength of the underground resistance movement, the *Istiqlal*, which eventually united and emerged as an Independent Party. With German and Spanish support it spread from Tangier to villages on the rim of the Sahara. Suppressive action provoked more and more rioting until at last, in 1955, even the die-hards on the Quai d'Orsay agreed that they had no option but to haul down the tricolour of the Protectorate.

'But why did you hang on for so long?' I had asked Général Guillaume when I met him in Europe.

He sighed. He paused. 'We were at the beck and call of about a hundred armchair politicians of the Colonial Party in the Chamber of Deputies,' he said. 'Some of them had never even set foot in North Africa. We foresaw what was inevitable many years earlier. They took no notice of us.'

Maxwell, one of the first foreigners to revisit Telouet, found that part of the *kasbah* had already been ruptured by cordite. Dead bodies of jackals, vultures and storks, the venerated bird of Morocco, littered the ground, covered in flies. He did not realise at the time that they had eaten locust swarms poisoned by means of a helicopter.

'What happened here?' he asked the Keeper of the Key, perhaps the same man we met there ourselves.

'I do not know,' he replied in basic French. 'The hand of Allah lies heavy on Telouet.'

The Blue People

MOUNTAINS OF THE MOON

GASTON DE Witte, Pango and I were hard on the tail of a young warthog which, by skilful driving, Gaston had managed to corner, leaving it no recourse other than to dive into a thicket of thorn-bushes and scrub about the size of a tennis court.

'Got the little bastard,' he said, chuckling.

We all got out. Pango, instructed by Gaston, brought along two rifles, a high-speed 30.06 which he carried, and for Gaston a light .22 which he reloaded with elongated red-painted shells.

'In there,' said Gaston, fondling one of them, 'is enough hexabarbitone to put that little fellow to sleep for at least an hour, but just in case papa or mama come out in a hurry one of us will hit it hard with *that*!' – and he pointed to the 30.06.

'You'd better stay near the wagon, but blow the horn and start shouting when we do.'

From opposite sides the two men began to encircle the thicket, shouting what I took to be obscenities in Flemish, gradually closing the range. Pango blasted off two shots in the air and out flew a flock of scarlet finches.

Suddenly he stopped and pointed excitedly. Gaston waddled round. With heart trouble and asthma he couldn't run, but he was nimble. He saw what Pango had seen, dropped down on to one knee and fired. A single shot.

The resultant squeals sounded as if the young hog had been trodden on. The noise gradually subsided. Pango was all for wading in but Gaston ordered him to bring some soft cotton rope which he coiled up into a lasso and threw, expertly.

They carried back a small, curiously dark-coloured warthog, wholly oblivious of what had been fired into its hairy backside.

'Now then,' said Gaston, unscrewing a square bottle of gin. 'What next? Look for some more snakes, or join the tourists in Rwanda? There'll be a lot of dancing and drumming.' *Outliers of Ruwenzori*

Pango drove, and with Porky cosily wrapped up in a large fishing net we bumped over the lightly wooded scrub with Gaston ever on the lookout for reptiles, especially snakes. He was not only extraordinarily gifted at spotting camouflaged creatures among foliage, many of which I had difficulty in making out even when he pointed to them; he could also 'read the ground', that is, identify impressions of reptilian prints left behind on wind-rippled sand or fine gravel. In an evocative phrase in Swahili, he had the ability to decipher *gazetti ya bundu*, the newspaper of the bush.

He found nothing worth catching that morning, but in a dried-up stream-bed, a *lugga*, it looked as if a water-pipe about a foot in diameter had recently been dragged from bank to bank. The spoor of a huge python. But why in a straight line? I should have expected a serpentine track. He smiled and rippled his fingers. Some large snakes, he told me, could 'walk' by opening and closing their scales.

Before Zaire achieved independence in 1960, Kigali as we saw it that afternoon was one of the principal cities of the Watutsi tribe, famous throughout Africa for their height – few are shorter than six feet – for their dancing and their drumming, and for the downright arrogance of their kings (*mwami*) and nobility.

To my surprise, one of them, seated, with his arms folded, was being pushed through the streets on a silver-plated bicycle by two servants who, Gaston told me, were little better than slaves. But why on a bicycle when he owned at least one Rolls-Royce? 'More people can see him that way,' he said.

Their subordinates, the stocky Bantu, probably arrived from West Africa but the Watutsi came down, originally, from somewhere in the region of the Upper Nile; nobody knows when and nobody knows why, except that they may have been seeking pasturage for their exceptionally long-horned cattle. Not so long bygone *mwamis* had a fearful reputation for elegant brutality. The people called them *nyagasani*, 'the lords, ever good, just and magnificent'. Their pleasures were expressed in *amategeko* (peremptory orders) manifested in massacres and fearful public tortures such as slow impalement. During periodic uprisings the Bantu literally and physically brought their lords and masters down to size by chopping their legs off. They also set fire to one of their over-opulent palaces, the one that was used for a film of *King Solomon's Mines*.

As soon as we drove through an archway of immense tusks I became aware of insistent, almost hypnotic pulsations like the electronic amplification of the beating of one's heart: now loud, now soft, almost feathery, but always rhythmical. Nothing of the staccato *tock*, *tock*, *tunk* of the

Lokele of the Cataracts about that sensuous throbbing. I began to tap my fingers, halving the beat. Gaston caught my tense look and smiled.

Explanations were cut short when we were 'attacked' by a tall, ferocious-looking fellow, black as a Zulu, gorgeously got up with feathers in his hair and a long 'spear' at the ready.

'Damned mendicants,' said Gaston, chucking a handful of francs on the ground.

Down we drove through tree-lined avenues, large classical administration buildings, sidewalk cafés and *boulangeries* which might have been anywhere in a sophisticated French or Belgian suburb, except for the presence of leopardskin-cloaked giants on silver-plated bicycles, net-veiled women, scowling servants and that fugal, counterpointed drumming, *da capo, encore et encore*.

We parked on the edge of Les Tambouriniers du Roi, where the cast jumped and cavorted to the rhythm of their ancient drums played by impassive men who either slapped the large skins hard with the palms of their hands or pecked at the smaller ones – six or seven inches in diameter – with the tips of their fingers. The marvel is that the sound

Watutsi dancers

of these fugues carried so far without mechanical amplification.

Gaston explained that the *corps de ballet* of perhaps a dozen dancers were re-enacting, with mimic gestures and huge leaps, what were ancient rituals being recalled: the Fearful Jurists, the Carriers of Fire, the Executioners and the Keepers of the Sacred Dreams.

We were sitting in the Land Rover. During one uncommonly quiet point in the performance when Gaston had slipped off to sleep, we heard a series of grunts and squeals which quickly turned into piercing screams, coming from the back of the vehicle. More grunts, squeaks and screams, and onlookers gathered around us. Pango grappled with the agitated warthog until it could be given another shot of dope. Within a quarter of an hour we were well out of town.

'What *are* you going to do with your young friend?' I asked Gaston.

He looked mysterious and grinned. 'I have a little plan which may amuse His Excellency,' he said. 'Perhaps we'll have a rehearsal tomorrow.'

The long day ended with a spectacular encounter with a pack of lycaons, the Cape hunting dogs, reckoned the most relentless, the most formidable pursuers of game in the whole of Africa south of the Sahara. Gaston sensed there were predators in our vicinity when we saw four gazelles racing along a ridge, as if running in front of a bush fire. They were followed by several bushbuck and some small antelopes, probably duikers. All were apparently terrified. At points of their flight they dislodged little cascades of stone that tinkled down upon us.

We stopped and he listened acutely. From afar came a long, eerie call like a whinny.

'Hunting dogs!' he said decisively. 'Now let's try and find out what they are up to.'

We drove to the top of the ridge where he got out and scanned the hummocky country through glasses. He pointed. 'There's a small pack on a hill over there, about a quarter of a mile away. Can't imagine what on earth they're doing. Better get nearer.'

He took the wheel and with that encircling movement we stopped within about a hundred yards of nine animals. They seemed totally oblivious to our presence. He handed me the glasses. They were mottled black, yellow and white with long rounded ears. Far from resembling fierce predators that have been known to attack lions around a kill, they were snapping and playing like fox cubs, though two or three gazed intently down on to the plain below.

After a time we saw a solitary dog racing up the hill towards them. All play ceased. There was a great deal of tail wagging and excited chatter and then all the animals ran off at top speed in the direction from which the scout had come.

We followed the animals in the Land Rover and as I wrote in my notebook at the time, 'There were about a dozen vultures flying overhead. I felt as if we were taking part in a medieval hunt with hawks and hounds.'

We came across a big gazelle lying on its side, completely disembowelled, presumably by the king dog and three others, perhaps the bitches, which had chased and pulled it down. It wasn't quite dead. One leg rose and fell feebly. Much to Gaston's surprise the pack we had followed didn't hurl themselves on the bloody corpse or squabble over their share. They stood aside expectantly, tense, licking their chops. The leader ate his fill and, with a big pelvic bone between his teeth, retired to the shelter of some bushes. As soon as he turned his back on the remains, the other animals slunk forward in twos and threes, in accordance with some in-built but hitherto unsuspected hierarchy of place. They ate until there was nothing left of that animal except the horns, part of the skull and a big patch of blood staining the grass.

On Gaston's assurance that hunting dogs had never been known to attack a human being, I ventured out to inspect the remains, covered, I admit, by two well-managed rifles.

As if they regarded me as an adjunct to the busy vultures, the dogs scarcely looked up. As far as he knew, said Gaston, this was the first time the pulling down, evisceration and near-complete ingestion of a Grant's gazelle (near sixty pounds) had been witnessed, recorded and timed: about twenty minutes.

As soon as he saw the official Parcs Nationaux envelope stamped *Important* on his dining table, Gaston let out an explosive '*Merde!*' and began to swear quietly but rapidly in what I took to be Flemish. 'This,' he said, 'is going to be yet another change in plans.' He read it and sighed. 'Just as I thought. Tomorrow we shall be going in different directions. His Excellency has decided to set off on a hunting trip with de Heinzelin and Camille Donis. They want me to look after the office in Bukavu, so they're sending a car with a man to drive you north.'

'But why can't I go back to Bukavu with you for a few days?'

'Listen, *mon ami*, you are like me, a victim of the Administration and orders from on high in Brussels, your Uncle Victor. He made out the schedule. In two days' time you are to be handed over to my good friend Jim Chapin, the famous ornithologist. He has a lovely house, not a *pied à terre* like this place. It's in the Virunga, where gorillas live among the volcanoes. *Eh bien!* Let's have a drink and see how Erymanthus is getting on. Pango's looking after him.'

187

'Erymanthus?'

He looked at me in mock surprise. 'Surely you've heard of the giant boar captured by Hercules?'

A bit of a mouthful, I thought, and suggested he should be called Harry, 'one of our favourite kings'.

Harry looked as if he was recovering from a three-star hangover which, come to think of it, I suppose he was but Pango assured us he'd drunk half a bucket of water and had sniffed around a tin plate of chopped vegetables, classic withdrawal symptoms.

He'd gone to sleep again in a close-wired chicken run with a small straw-lined shed for the night.

The man who'd handled yards of pythons and mambas had a deep respect for what he called 'those bloody ants' – warrior ants – about which he muttered as he gently fingered Harry's exposed parts, especially his backside where he'd hit him with his doped *fléchette*.

'About those ants,' he said, 'I have a rather curious story to tell but I suppose I'd better phone Bukavu first. They've probably changed their minds again by now. Get another drink. Look over my books. *Chakula* [food] in about an hour.'

Over supper I learned a great deal about the Parks Department. His Excellency was in effect the vice-president of the whole country. He was much in favour of increasing their revenue from tourism, second only to their mineral resources in the Katanga. Uncle Victor was at best a late convert to the idea. 'Like me,' said Gaston, 'he is *au fond* an ecologist and at heart he regards tourists as parasites interested primarily in that fossilised stuff we saw this afternoon. In between times they like to see a few animals from the safety of a seat in an autobus among the companions they are familiar with at home. What are we to do? This is where you come in, my friend. We need to strike a balance between an enormous open-air zoo where familiar birds and quite a few animals such as primates wait for the coaches to come in to be fed and photographed, and land management, which is expensive.

'Did Camille tell you about affairs in the Ituri, one of the small tributaries of the big river at Stan? By God! What a smell! Just about everything had died over a length of about six miles: hundreds of hippos, elephants, wildebeest, zebras, even crocodiles. An enormous epidemic of anthrax, which in acute cases can kill vertebrates, including man, in a couple of hours. In this case poachers had killed off most of the predators for their valuable skins. The animals, especially the hippos, should have been thinned out ruthlessly before the place became overpopulated. But for years Uncle Victor wouldn't have it. He kept on talking about letting nature take her own course. He found out when it was too late to do much about it.'

'So you think everything has its place in the web of life,' I said. 'What *Harbingers of death*

189

*Lobelia: botanical
big game*

about those bloody warrior ants you are so worried about?'

He laughed. 'Well, yes, I can tell you a case where they once saved a man's life.

'In the Kagera Park, years ago, I met a wanade hunter who wouldn't have been alive if it wasn't for the fact that once a soldier ant closes its pincer-like jaws on a piece of skin, it's very difficult to prise them apart. I had been employing the fellow as a guide and at supper one night I noticed his upper arm was furrowed by a scar which stretched from his wrist to just below his shoulder blade.

'The story, as he told it, was that he'd been walking through a forest track miles from anywhere when a leopard sprang out and pinned his dog to the ground. The fellow lunged at it with his spear and wounded it, but before the animal made off it raked him with its claws. Blood poured from a large flap of skin nearly the length of his arm. Realising he was in danger of bleeding to death the hunter tore up his shirt into a cradle strip of bandage and looked around until he found a trail of army ants. By holding the big-jawed specimens over the edges of the wound one by one he induced them to close their pincers on the flap of skin in such a way that they clasped the edges together. Once the bodies had been nipped off he was left with a row of "stitches" composed of ants' jaws.

'And now we'd better be off to bed,' said Gaston. 'I'll just go out for a minute to see if Harry's comfortable. Tomorrow he'll be the proudest little hog in the Parc Albert.'

Clearly Gaston was up to something.

Yohanni, a sullen-faced Somali, turned up with a brightly polished Land Rover before we'd finished breakfast. In one sharp word, '*Limbika*', spoken peremptorily, Gaston told him to wait.

'A bit thick between the ears and only understands commands. You know enough Swahili to keep him in order. He's fairly honest – if he's watched. No loans. No credit. He's already received his daily allowance. Don't allow him into a *duka* [store] unless you go with him, and pocket the ignition key *whenever* you leave the wagon together.'

'He's apt to drive too fast. If he does, shout *Kwenda poli-poli*! Any sign of insubordination, threaten to tell his boss, Donis, the *Bwana m'Kubwa*.

'Here's a map of your route. It's up to Chapin's place above Lake Edward in the Virunga. If you start soon you can do it fairly easily in one day, but if you want to stretch your legs, stop at Ishango. Marvellous view of the volcanoes and the peaks of the Ruwenzori. There's a guest-house there run by an amiable Belgian woman. Can't remember her name but I think she'll remember me. She's from St Hubert in

Walloon country, where the famous rose painter, Redouté, came from. Make a fuss of her and give her my regards.'

'Gaston,' I said, holding out my hand, 'I wish you were coming with me. Can't tell you how much you've taught me.'

'Wait!' he said. 'You haven't seen Harry yet. You won't know him.'

We walked round to the back where the young boar had just finished his breakfast and was trotting up and down.

Explorer Hillaby

192

Most wild pigs, young and old, hold their thin tails up in the air like a curlicue or a question mark. I don't know how Gaston had managed to fasten the thing on securely, but from the top three inches of young Harry's tail there floated one of the small black, yellow and red flags which adorned the Governor's limousines when he was out on official business. Gaston said he proposed to release the animal in the residential gardens when His Excellency came up to Bukavu with Camille Donis the following week.

We cruised along the eastern shore of Lake Kivu, characterised by nothing except eucalyptus trees and troops of baboons apparently trying to play 'last across the road'. By some elaborate swerves in the wrong direction on at least two occasions it became clear that Yohanni was trying to run them down.

I said, '*Angalia* (Take care)!' When that didn't work I shouted, '*Poli-poli* (Go slower)!' At this he slipped into second gear, which brought us down to about 10 mph. I had an old soldier to deal with, and resorted to old-fashioned hand signals accompanied by ferocious glares.

By wafting my hands upwards slowly as if to get the full aroma of a plate of curried rice and pork, and conversely wafting them downwards, I managed to get it into his thick head that I wanted him to go a *bit* slower or a *bit* faster. Beyond that I said nothing but *M'zuri* (good) or *M'baya* (bad), and said it in a wholly impassive voice. What else was necessary? I found out about half an hour before lunch.

The road had become little better than a cinder track that climbed steadily, in a series of generous loops, through thickets of tree ferns and rocky ground ablaze with *Kniphofia*, known in suburban English gardens as red-hot pokers, and in the United States as flame lilies. No baboons. Why so common on the tarmac surfaces around Kivu? Cadgers?

An immense buffalo, several jackal-like dogs without the sloping backs of hyenas, and small antelopes on springs merely glanced at us before they skipped or trotted off. Most of all I should have liked to know the names of birds quite unfamiliar to me, such as the red-headed finches and long-tailed flycatchers that danced in the shadows of tall, flowering trees on stilts. In between short rests to relieve ourselves – and the engine – I scribbled down questions to ask Chapin. Yohanni had next to nothing to say except that he wanted his food (*chakula*). I told him to wait (*limbika*).

During one such halt, about five minutes, just outside a dilapidated village, I came back unexpectedly to find him arguing with an old man over the price of two proffered fish about the size of herrings. I got into the Land Rover. Yohanni grabbed the fish and drove off. The old man screamed and ran after us. It took a few seconds for me to remember to shout the word for 'Stop!' twice.

Under threat of reporting him to the Big Chief, I made him drive back, and it didn't improve interpersonal relationships when I ordered him to pay the man double what he'd originally asked (about tuppence), and then lost our way by some inexpert map reading at a critical and unsignposted junction of tracks.

By sheer good luck the one I chose had recently been resurfaced, but then we began to climb steadily along a dead straight road which, for some quite unobvious reason, had been cut through a vast tropical forest, the first I had ever seen. Its immensity could be gauged by a broad gap used for construction machinery where I stopped, walked about a hundred yards, and from the rim of a quarry of black rock gazed down on a slope of trees extending as far as the eye could see to a far distant haze.

Some odd arboreal giants overtopped the rest, playing solo parts in the mass of vegetable symphony. No flowers except a touch of scarlet from unripe cactus and other prickly shrubs; not a note of any colour but a sullen green, a very dark monotonous green which gave the landscapes the solemn tranquillity of our northern coniferous forests as seen from surrounding hills.

Before I rejoined the sullen Yohanni, still patting his stomach, I walked to the perimeter of that quarry and was rewarded by an intermittent flash, winking like a heliograph to the south east and not far away. Surely Lake Edward. By accident we were on the right course.

The fellow looked so damned miserable that against all instructions I gave him a small bottle of beer and a packet of sandwiches, which my good friend Gaston had provided against emergencies.

After another hour or so when, for several reasons, we stopped close to a wooden-bridged stream, I told him to check oil, gas and water, gave him a couple of Belgian candy bars to which he had become addicted, and with the ignition key safely in my pocket went off, alone for once, to explore briefly the principal inhabitants of one of those rapidly declining areas of the world, the fringe of the immense primary forest, the land of giant trees.

Armed only with a *panga*, an outsize in bill-hooks, I found a few specimens which, like those around the quarry, had been isolated from their neighbours by the building of the road. Behind them, with prickly scrub at their feet, absolutely impenetrable – except to pygmies, as I was soon to discover – lay a botanical wilderness.

The biggest trees appeared to be upheld from the base by a thick fasces of vertical branches which resembled the folds of a foot-length dress. Others seemed to be supported by sturdy flying buttresses which *Eventual destination* gave the impression that the giants were walking. All were hung about

194

with dangling bell-ropes of lianas, dead straight, almost without leaves, emerging from the darkness above.

Incautiously I pulled one, slowly, as though tolling the last bell before eight o'clock Mass.

Down fell two or three small bright green snakes, several centipedes, a profusion of insects, cicadas, mantids and, worst of all by far, a shower of black and red ants. Thanks to the angle at which I had pulled the thing I got off lightly, but had been stung about the neck and arms, and I sprinted back to the wagon to strip off and wash in the stream.

Yanni, as I called him when he behaved himself, looked on with badly disguised amusement. Thank God he hadn't seen me doing something I shall never do again. With my scalp, ears, eyelids and chest still burning despite liberal sploshes of an ointment containing a powerful antihistamine, we rolled on for mile after mile through giant tree-scapes towards which my curiosity had notably diminished.

Without using that overworn phrase 'the heart of darkness', how can one describe a realm which must have been growing untouched for many centuries? The absence of any ray of sunlight gave it the look of being sunk in sleep, a look of hopeless sadness. All the leaves were shiny and firm like those of rhododendron, laurel and evergreen oak. There was nothing like our northern hazel, beech or willow, soft and silk-like, porous to the light and giving a golden-green haze to the rays of the sun that pass through them. They make copses and glades abodes of evocative mystery, fit for Artemis, Lady of the Wild Things, and her attendant dryads. Primary equatorial forests, you could easily imagine, are fit only for devils.

The road began to rise steeply; the giants gradually thinned out into a mixture of trees and scrub interspersed with occasional plantations. On either side the road was flanked by the reddish trunks of tall eucalyptus planted at such regular intervals that the rapid alternation of light and shadow had a hypnotic effect. I began to feel tired and slightly dizzy.

Suddenly, so suddenly, around a sharp bend of the road we were flooded by light, as if we'd emerged from a half-lit crypt. Below us was the immense surface of Lake Edward, and up in the sky to the north the snow-capped peaks of my ultimate destination, the Ruwenzori, the Mountains of the Moon. 'And I saw a new heaven and a new earth: for the first heaven and the first earth were passed away. . . .'

Rhetorical stuff written that night after a sumptuous dinner as the only guest of Madame Couverte, *patronne* of l'Hôtel Ishango, a guest-house that wasn't doing too well despite a subsidy from the Parks Department.

She greeted me fulsomely – 'Ah M'sieu' – *il y a un dépêche pour vous – c'est un peu compliqué.*

'Ah! pardon me. It is from our mutual friend M. le Baron Gaston de Witte. He regrets very much to say that a half-hour after you left this morning he received a telephone blow from M. James Chapin who was returning to his home this day and hoped to see you there. Also M. de Heinzelin is ready to take you up to see the volcanoes. M. le Baron thinks you should telephone him. I have the number. Shall I call him? No, first, *peut-être un apéritif?*'

Disguising despondency with a toothy smile, I asked what could be better.

During much tinkering about with bottles Madame Couverte repeated what Gaston had already told me, that she came from St Hubert, named after the Blessed Apostle of the Ardennes. The hotel was littered with distinctly faded prints of Redouté's roses. She and M. le Baron had much in common, she told me. I knew that too. I could smell the *genièvre* at a range of three paces. She poured me out a large one.

A pity about the famous American, M. Chapin. He had looked in twice on his way to *le marais* with his pygmy friend. That threw me completely, but I let it pass.

After supper I got through to Gaston, who was somewhere between choleric and very apologetic. Damned Parcs again! As he saw it I should make for Chapin's place at L'wiro down the big road on the west side of the lake, where de Heinzelin would pick me up in two days' time. He gave me directions. If any trouble, he'd pick me up there himself. 'Don't forget Ishango,' he said. '*Meilleures salutations et bonne chance.*'

After flowing south out of Lake Albert and encircling the Ruwenzori massif as if unsure where to go, the Semliki River runs into the top – that is, the southern end – of Lake Edward at Ishango, showing fairly clearly that both lakes were once the outermost feeders of the Nile. What upended that extremity of the Great Rift Valley was the chain of volcanoes to which I was heading that glorious morning.

To Yohanni's marked discontent I got him on to a small viewing platform above the river an hour after sunrise. There I indulged in two hours of crocodile, hippo, elephant and bird-watching.

Gaston had called the place marvellous. A stronger epithet is necessary. Perhaps prelapsarian, a word I picked up from that reverent nineteenth-century naturalist, Canon William Buckland. He, like Archbishop Ussher, believed that Genesis had taken place on a certain day in the year 4,000 BC, probably a Sunday. In its broadest sense the word means as life was in the Garden of Eden before the Fall. There was a sense of amity, of contentment in that vast expanse of sand, marshes, water and grassy islands below us.

Half a dozen crocodiles were lying side by side, sunning themselves, each nose almost touching the scarcely moving river. Mutual protection. They can't turn round quickly.

A sudden dive and they all dived. Otherwise an individual, perhaps bored, slid into the water, voluptuously. Egrets on their backs did sentinel duty.

Elephants up to their knees in the water, probing with their trunks, and hippos, almost submerged, seemed to be getting along fine. Their enormous heads emerged here and there, but only to make farty noises or open their mouths and roar, lazily, *oo-ah, oo-ah, oo-ah*, and then sink down again almost apologetically.

There were hosts of birds, but I could only put a name to those indistinguishable from their European counterparts – flamingoes, stilts, avocets and skittery little waders resembling sanderlings that run about near the water like clockwork mice. Perhaps they were the same species at the southern limit of their annual migration. They certainly acted in the same way as those I know well. In the air all the plovers I have ever seen play with the slightest of wind, toying with it, rolling over, not caring how it strikes them. But, the flight over, they glide down, landing delicately, scarcely seeming to touch the ground until with a little run they come to rest. For an instant the wings are uplifted, then swept back in the manner of a gallant bow, and they settle with a little shiver of ecstasy. Whoever invented the word grace, in its secular sense, said Aldo Leopold, must have noticed the wing-folding of plovers.

At Ishango I learned that elephants, the symbol of giantism, exhibit, both strongly, paternalism and a delicacy of their own in their stately tread and feeding habits. One old tusker emerged from a thicket of trees about a hundred yards away to our left, leading what I took to be his extended family, some twenty animals in all, towards the pools and marshy surrounds of the incoming river. They moved as if in a state procession, almost nose to tail, not wavering from the sinuous track carefully sounded out by the old bull. Although he never seemed to hesitate for more than a second or two, it was clear by the way he extended his forefeet, first one and then the other, that he was testing the ground carefully to see if it would bear his weight, which was so much greater than the others. Some of the *totos*, the youngsters, seemed a bit impatient, but if they strayed more than two or three yards out of line, they got a slap across the ears from the trunk of the nearest adult.

Evidently the old man had far more faith in the solidity of the river-bed than the dangerous marsh, for he splashed across confidently and heaved himself out on to a large grassy island. The others followed, in no particular order. Discipline was mostly over and tension relaxed, especially among the younger set. They were like children who had been led into a playground, and the *totos*, like children everywhere,

became mischievous and apt to wander off on their own. Then they all formed into smaller groups, presumably more immediate families, and got down to the serious business of the morning.

They had a fine choice of food and took it in different ways. Some were homely grass-eaters, but through powerful glasses I could see that the older animals favoured the young sprouts on the muddy banks of the river. They hauled out the plants, roots and all, sometimes biting off only the succulent parts, as we should with asparagus, sometimes carefully washing the whole plant before scrunching it up, roots and all. Other animals, up to their bellies in the shallows, seemed to offer similar treatment to the equatorial equivalent of watercress.

As the sun rose higher, the pack, still under the leadership of the old man, trooped off to another island bordered by leafy trees, and we managed to follow them along a narrow track. Here they took their second course consisting of succulent shoots which they pulled down from the trees, belching and farting and using the branches as fly-whisks.

Others, perhaps mostly females, did themselves up, sucking up water and flicking it over their heads and shoulders, like a woman using a *Suspicious croc.*

powder puff. The *totos*, nuisances as ever, wandered off until they were herded back by some testy old aunt in the role of baby-watcher. I noticed that some of the kids bore scars about their backsides, and one had almost lost its tail. Evidence of an unsuccessful attack by lion or leopard? Only the vultures and screaming fish eagles, ever present on the lakes and rivers, could have witnessed such an attack.

Elephants were much on my mind as Yanni drove me, as fast as I would let him, towards the Chapins' place at L'wiro. Surely they were the most gentlemanly, the most good-natured creatures on earth? Gaston had told me that if they turned up late at a large communal water-hole occupied by other animals, they would hang about, awaiting their turn. He had seen this happen when the water was being used as a bath by several buffaloes more intent on splashing about than quenching their thirst. When the buffaloes had fouled the place up and lumbered

Happy families

200

off, the elephants (five) inspected the far side of the pool where the water was less soupy than the rest, then knelt down, like Muslims at prayer, extended their trunks as far as possible and drank for a few minutes before wading in and indulging in noisy toilet activities.

But if they are molested or injured, or – worse – killed, Gaston said, they become obsessed to a point of hysteria. With one animal on either side of their inert companion, the biggest tuskers usually try to prise it to its feet and support it. They have been known to stand on guard overnight and then, sensing it is dead, the big males may start a war dance, breaking and tearing at everything to hand, usually vegetable. They throw leaves and branches up in the air, trumpeting loudly, indulging in what ethologists call displacement activity, a product of conflicting emotions, such as attack or fright.

Ruth, wife of Jim Chapin, one of the Lords of the High Courts of International Ornithology, was waiting to greet me. 'Couldn't bear to think we'd missed you twice.' she said. 'Sit down and I'll fix you something. Jim's out after some goddamn bee-eater just arrived. He'll be back in an hour.'

She offered me a dry Martini. I said I'd prefer a Scotch with a lot of water. After my second eyebrow-lifter I realised I was in the presence of a type not uncommon in the tropics, a warm, lovable, outspoken expatriate wholly devoted to her husband's activities.

'How come you're so close to Van Straelen?' she asked. I told her.

'Not a man to fall out with,' she said. 'With the exception of Gaston and de Heinzelin, who've got money of their own, he scares the pants off most of the Belgian wardens and biologists.'

'But not you, I take it?'

She laughed. 'In the first place he gets us for free. Jim's been collecting birds for the American Museum of Natural History for nearly half a century and for a lot of that time we've been right here in the Congo. Secondly, what with the famous peacock and I don't know how many other species, he's brought quite a lot of fame to the Parks, and fame means money from their government.'

'How long do you intend to stay here?'

'We're off pretty soon. We don't like the way things are going.'

'Kitiwala?'

She sniffed. 'That's what they all say. Jim doesn't believe it. There's no unity among the tribes. Many of them hate each other's guts. The Belgians put in puppet chiefs who can be fired. Nobody knows the names of the real chiefs, except the political agents.'

'From Brussels?'

'Listen, John, all I've told you is strictly off the record. Jim always says I talk too much. Anyway here he is, with the Little Corporal.'

A thin, elderly man with the soft voice of a New Englander held out his hand. He apologised for missing me at Ishango: not for the first time somebody had got their dates screwed up, he said. The original plan was for us all to go up there together with de Heinzelin on our way to Epulu in pygmy country.

'What about the bee-eater?' asked Ruth.

'Only got a glimpse,' he said. 'Looks like a sub-species of *nubicus*.'

For the rest of that afternoon and until de Heinzelen arrived to take me up into the volcanoes the next day, Jim Chapin, assuming I knew far more about dickie-birdology than I did, chucked scientific names at me as if I were a professional systematist. The bird he was referring to was one of that colourful genus of *merops* called carmine bee-eaters.

His spacious garden, planted with flaming coral trees (*Erythrina*), was the haunt of small, hovering birds with slender, curved bills (*Nectarinia*) and at least twenty other species including social weaver birds which resembled finches, but which, he assured me, were members of the European super-family of sparrows. This wholly baffled me, so I turned to the famous peacock which he had discovered.

'Quite a long story, that,' he said. 'Better ask Ruth.'

He was anxious to show me one of his favourite groups of birds, the honey-guides: *Indicator indicator congensis* in his language. These birds have developed the remarkable habit of guiding human beings and badger-like animals to the nests of wild bees in order to feed on the honeycomb and grubs when the nests are chopped out. This makes them distinctly unpopular with the natives, who keep bees and sometimes put their own 'hives', hollow logs, up in trees. 'Don't know how we can get round that one,' he said.

At half-past six it grew dark with the sudden finality which marks the end of the day in the Congo and we moved back towards the house. On the way he took me into his museum, his laboratory and what he called the 'skin shed', where Caporali, the cheerful 'Little Corporal', was at work.

'A pure-bred pygmy from Epulu. Been with me twelve years. Took two years to train him. Now I can trust him with the best specimens I get. He can also shoot straight. Number twelve dust shot at close range. And he can climb a tree like a monkey, which is useful.'

The Chapins lived on a carefully chosen volcanic slope with a stepped garden that afforded sanctuary to several groups of birds which interested Jim. It followed that the low, prickly bushes attracted shrikes and the like; these were overlooked by flame trees where there were three species of ever-hovering sunbirds, then on up to a thick palisade of bamboo which attracted the haunters of tall grass, and, very occasionally, he told me, an inquisitive young gorilla.

Twilight brought neither peace nor quiet. What with the *poink, poink,*

Giant heathers

poink of banana bats and the whistle of nightjars with long streamers trailing from their wings, it gave the impression of a Chinese orchestra tuning up.

The next day we were out again and I was introduced to close on a hundred birds I'd never seen before – there are over a thousand in the Congo. By far the most spectacular was a crowned eagle which swooped down on to the skull of a Colobus monkey sitting rather stupidly on the flat top of a palm tree, and carried it off, flailing its limbs and screaming.

Our quiet search for honey-guides was brought to a noisy halt by the arrival of a clapped-out truck and two jeeps into which had been squeezed sixteen porters and three or four armed guards who were all enjoying themselves hugely. The procession was led by Jean de Heinzelin in an almost new Land Rover, a gift, he said, from the Governor of the Congo.

'What for?' I asked him.

'Sheer gratitude for my company. We were students together at Louvain.'

About Jean there was something both in manner and appearance that put you in mind of that superb, that most laconic of French actors, Louis Jouvet. He bowed slightly to Madame Chapin, embraced her and then shook hands with her husband as if they hadn't met for years. He regretted that we had to leave in half an hour but, as he explained, he was obliged to pick up supplies on the way.

Nyiragongo is one of about a dozen volcanoes in the west-to-east Virunga chain not very far north of Lake Kivu. As I had been watching smoke belch out of it at intervals for days, sometimes so thickly it obscured the sun, I couldn't understand why Jean had brought along twenty men to accompany us. Couldn't we at least get up there in about a day? I put the question to him as we began to zig-zag upwards through a thick forest clinging precariously to the sides of a cliff.

'Definitely not,' he said as he swerved to avoid a troop of baboons engaged in taking a dust bath. 'You'll see why not in about half an hour when we'll be looking across to the lava fields.'

'What's the story about Jim Chapin and the peacocks?' I asked.

'Detective Simenon turns to ornithology. The discovery of treasure that nobody else had even heard of! Jim spotted an old and tattered head-dress of a Banande chief in the ornithological museum near Brussels and it included plumage from a peacock, a family of birds unknown in Africa. Jim recognised a few critical feathers and tracked the remnants of the chief's tribe back to the Epulu district, where we hoped to be going in a few days' time. He went out there and offered rewards for information about the bird. Within three years he'd seen a few pairs himself, and he named the species *Afropavo congensis*. It's now bred in a few zoos.'

Jean rounded a bend, stopped, pointed dramatically to a platform of rock and said, 'Walk up there and take a look. We've got to get through that lot to pick up supplies before tomorrow night. Don't know whether we shall be able to make it.'

A glimpse of hell as Dante saw it but without souls, good or bad. *Nothing* except seemingly endless corrugations of grey-black lava, wrinkled, folded, some fields torn apart into grotesque canyons. All stuff vomited out of the chain of volcanoes ahead of us.

Alone among them, Nyiragongo, our objective, coughed petulantly, blowing out smoke rings like flying saucers. Earth tremors, too, showing, as Jean put it – in Ki-swahili – *Karibu amekwisha kufa*, she was not quite dead.

'Come on,' he said, '*allons-y*, the cannibals are getting restless.'

'Why do you always call her *she*?' I asked, as he pointed out other volcanoes. Mikeno, the highest (14,600 ft); the haunt of most of the Congolese gorillas, snow-capped Karisimbi; Sabinio. We couldn't see the other four big ones.

'Because there was a beautiful woman, the wife of a Wasongole chief. Stanley is reputed to have said she was the most graceful dancer he had ever seen, and he'd visited Bali before coming to Africa. You've seen Rwanda dancers put on for tourists and they're good.

'I think there's a gene for eurhythmics. It's certainly present in Western Russia, and where did it come from? Muhavura, the volcano behind Sabinio, pretty close to Belgian Congo, Ruandi-Urundi and Uganda. What about a new theory of evolution, a mixture of tribes through communal dancing, and the spread of that cult through those who hopped about like apes and were scarcely able to bear their own weight?

'What happened to aboriginal mankind when it crossed the Bering Straits and slipped into slit-eyed *Esquimaux* forever squatting over holes in the ice, or fighting each other as your Redmen did? Or puffing pot, making baskets and speaking Mojave, closely related to Athapascan linguistics? Did you ever hear of any of them *dancing* to rhythms apart from those imported from Spain?'

'But tell me about Nyiragongo.'

'She became too democratic. She danced with her husband's men – or strangers – and legend says one of them tried, or maybe succeeded, in raping her, and she threw herself into the crater which was named after her. Forever smoking or vomiting out lava and fire, it became the symbol of damned souls. Those without sin – and I've yet to meet them – live forever on the summit of Karisimbi whose breasts now and again are modestly draped with snow.'

Jean waved his convoy to a standstill and we looked at the lava at close quarters. What are the immense lumps, some ten or fifteen feet high, resembling a mass of coiled serpents? I asked. He chipped off a piece and examined it through a strong lens.

'Quite recent stuff. Look at that mica. Could be from an eruption I watched from start to finish during three months of 1954. Streams of lava pouring into Lake Kivu sounded like half a dozen space rockets being launched. The shallows at the top end boiled, so the natives got their fish already cooked.

'She'd been suffering from indigestion for eighteen months before that. Blocked pipes. She coughed out what you call the serpents, followed by one hell of a bang and a mushroom cloud like an atomic bomb. It wasn't safe to come up here. These things like cannonballs flattened at the bottom spun round perhaps two or three thousand feet in the air when they were softer than putty, then spattered down on to old hard lava.

'If you could bore through this lot easily you'd screw up a core with bits at the bottom as old as the Rift Valley, the biggest crack on the earth's surface, some sixty million years old.'

A low platform further up the slope looked like an old railway embankment. 'That used to be the road from Goma to the first rest-house on Nyiragongo; now it's a corridor of lava covered with millions of tons of cinders. Supposed to be dangerous.'

An exuberant schoolboy lurked behind the sophisticated exterior of Jean de Heinzelin. He couldn't trust the cannibals to get over the thing in their clapped-out trucks, so he rerouted them to allow us to try the causeway on our own and clip at least thirty miles off the first part of the journey. As a bonus he thought we might get a glimpse of his friend Bertie.

We made it in four anxious hours with, now and again, wheels spinning up to their hubs on smoking tyres. My task was to walk ahead armed with a bamboo pole six feet long with a pointed steel ferrule to poke into the cinders: 'If it comes out charred or starts to smoke we'd better have another think,' he said. I said yes, bleakly.

He looked with the curiosity of a geologist at a small spire of steam about a hundred yards ahead. 'Not encouraging. Out you go,' he said.

I probed gently. Very little resistance. I shoved harder. No change at a two- or three-feet depth though I thought – perhaps imagined – that the sound of the pressure increased. I pulled out the probe, considerably relieved, and tried again at varying distances from the vent. I struck hard rock (lava) not far below the surface. Surveyor Hillaby smugly reported his prowess.

We met a small bed of scrubby bushes with some exotic flowers among them. Jean carried a *panga* and slashed about a few inches below the surface until he began to unearth large, charred bones.

'A big buck must have sunk in and got incinerated, although God

Giant St John's wort

knows what brought it up here. This is all the vultures left: bacteria and nitrogen have brought the cinders back to life.' He scanned the low hills nearby. 'We've made it! Haven't been up here for years, but I know exactly where we are.'

Powerful field glasses brought close a golgotha of carbonised trees with stuff growing at their feet and, beyond that, stratified greenery topped by the bare blunt snout of a smoking volcano, Nyiragongo.

'Who's Bertie?' I asked belatedly as we swung up into an unexpected scrub remarkable for a small herd of grazing zebra and wildebeest among eucalyptus trees.

'He lives on a plantation just above the guest-house. We ought to be there in about an hour.'

Four tails like bell-ropes hung down from one of the trees. I took the field glasses. *'Voilà des lions.'*

'Non, des lionnes,' Jean corrected, and one of them obligingly stalked down slowly and majestically, as if aware of her condition.

Our arrival at the guest-house, Camp des Bruyères, 7,600 feet, just before sundown was nicely marked by a subterranean explosion that shook down the fibrous nests of some extremely angry wasps just above the door, and shook me considerably. 'The lady,' said Jean, 'is suffering from indigestion today. But don't worry. I've taken her pulse at monthly intervals from the far side of this slope for nearly four years, and I can assure you she's slipping into a state of graceful decline. If not, your Uncle Victor will almost certainly find someone to replace me.'

207

Near her time

Inside the double walls of what looked like roughly hewn rosewood was a huge, polished table, chairs, cupboards and five bunks, all of the same wood. Jean rubbed the surface gently and smelt his fingers. 'Know what that is?' I shook my head. 'From giant heathers, *bruyères*, which grow up to fifty feet around here. They make the best pipes for smokers.' He went off with the little Batwa cook-housekeeper to see what we could have for dinner.

Eland ribs under a thin layer of cranberry sauce, sweet potatoes and boiled lichens served with *Côtes du Rhône* decanted from gallon flasks

208

flown in from Belgium to Bukavu. The Belgians lived well. From outside came a shrill trumpeting noise and crashing about.

'Elephants,' said Jean, sucking a rib between his fingers and thumbs. 'Gentle creatures if left alone. Wish they'd push off, though, I'd like you to hear the hyraxes. The place swarms with them. You haven't heard them? Tree rats. The conies of the Bible. But this is the arboreal species, *Dendrohyrax*, favourite food of our leopards. Now there's a creature to keep away from. *Formidable*! Camille Donis shot one, 140 kilos — what's that in your funny lingo? About 300 pounds! The skin's still on Madame's bedroom floor. Whisper the word *chu'wee* to Goli, the cook here, and he'll climb up the wall. I wouldn't go out at night without a choked twelve bore; that would stop anything at thirty feet.'

The talk turned to the edibility of game. Eland, hung for at least a week, was the best, in his opinion. Depended where your cook cut it. Possibly wild boar was more reliable than anything else, which reminded me that Gaston had . . . yes, he'd heard the story. Apparently the Governor wasn't much amused. Said it was the Flemish sense of humour. Old antagonisms *et cetera*. Insult to Belgium. Goli refreshed the decanter.

Then could one eat all wild game? He thought for a moment. Depended on how hungry you were. George Adamson, stranded by a gale on Lake Rudolf without either gun or rod, climbed up a palm tree and lived for a couple of days on the addled eggs of a pair of vultures. But George was a *m'chezo*, a freak. As for himself, apart from the liver and the kidneys, *toujours de bon goût*, most of the gazelles would at least make a good ragout. The exception was waterbuck, which tasted putrid. Perhaps its natural protection. It paddles about in water where even crocodiles won't touch it. Native fishermen know this, and when they wade in themselves they sometimes wear pants made of its skin. Anyhow it's time for bed. Let's go out and have a look at the old lady.

A breath-catching spectacle. The ash-laden clouds above the boiling lava were pinkish, but shot through and through by unceasing volcanic lightning, sometimes in rapid horizontal flashes, then in oblique forked streaks, or again in tortuous lines like fiery serpents.

'Isn't it dangerous to get up on to the crater with that going on above your head?'

'No, it's cloud-to-cloud stuff, and those clouds are at least 2,000 feet above the rim.'

Before we settled down, the hyraxes began to whistle. At first a mere breathy murmur mounted in scale and intensity as if they were trying to outdo each other until it became impossible to distinguish between the individuals, a cicada-like chorus.

At the sound of a deep, sepulchral cough, everything suddenly became quiet.

Lakeside groundsels

A yawn, and a sleepy voice from the next bed said, 'A leopard on the prowl. Tell Goli to go out and scare the damned thing away.'

Dawn at a clearing in a tropical forest is an occasion for an orchestra of bird-song and calls – mostly raucous, particularly if coucals, touracos and hornbills are in the vicinity; one of the latter can grunt like a dissatisfied lion. Doves are the most melodious and the mourning dove by far the saddest of all, often lamenting, phonetically, that 'my *ma-ma* is dead: my *pa-pa* is dead and my heart goes *doo, doo, doo, doo*'. There must have been at least two on the roof and there couldn't have been a more pleasant awakening until pandemonium broke out. Hooters hooted, two empty fuel drums were tossed out of the truck amid shouts and cheerful squeals from twenty hungry men. The cannibals had turned up.

A fine band we looked, I think, as we trudged up towards Camp Two at Mushamangaro, the last before the final scramble towards the rim of a crater at a little over 11,000 feet. Again I was leading with the bamboo pole, this time to test the deep bogs which might be up to twenty feet in depth. Jean, in his role of technical adviser, was wearing a white solar topi – probably the last in Central Africa – and walked

Ruwenzu means rain

close on my heel. Thereafter, in single file, came the rest of the all-black company, including three they'd picked up on the way as local guides, all barefooted and each carrying over fifty pounds weight on his head. Why so much?

'If we are forced to stop anywhere we can set up camp almost immediately,' explained Jean. 'Anyway, we'll stop pretty soon and with any luck you'll meet my friend Bertie.'

The company were ordered to wait on a hill while he and I slipped down to a heavily palisaded compound round a small lake. Jean suggested that I should stay behind for a few minutes. I heard the trumpeting and the sound of whips before, from under a tree, there emerged the finest, the largest, the rarest elephant I have ever seen or am ever likely to see. This was Bertie, named after the Parc Albert.

The principal stud bull of the Station de Domestication de Gangela na Bodio – already the father of forty *totos* – was out for a bit of relaxation. I have forgotten his dimensions, but his tusks almost touched the ground. Unlike the usual African elephant, *Loxodonta africana*, this huge example of the normally small Ruwenzori sub-species (*cyclotis*) has relatively circular ears and is now so rare that it's in danger of becoming extinct. Jean seemed annoyed about what he called 'those bloody krauts', the group in charge of the beasts, and promised to tell me more later. We soldiered on.

When travelling Indian file on a narrow path through thick tropical forest, the custom is for anyone who sees anything potentially dangerous to warn those following by pointing left or right, slapping his buttock quietly or vigorously according to the circumstances. Potentially thick bog merits no more than a patter akin to polite applause at the end of an indifferent concert. The same goes for large droppings: elephant, rhino or buffalo – the latter, like horse shit, the worst by far since the depositors are much given to cryptic attack. The question for those capable of reading the bush is: are the droppings dry, moist or, most ominous of all, steamy?

I thought I'd scored at least a point or two by spotting several feet of a ribbon snake (harmless enough, Gaston had assured me) draped around a flame tree. Then came a chimpanzee's nest near the top of a giant heather from which emerged a reddish, hairy arm – the tenant, presumably doing some odd DIY jobs to the roof.

This interested Jean, who mentioned a very rare species, a solitary, non-gregarious chimpanzee called the *Bonobo* which – he had heard – was closer to man in its blood group than any other primate and was being relentlessly pursued by the unscrupulous directors of two international chemical corporations, to the point where it could well be wiped out. From it they were trying to manufacture a vaccine against poliomyelitis, the dreaded infantile paralysis.

Bertie

The cannibals weren't in the least interested in the chimp and didn't even bother to look up: it was as if I'd pointed out a London bus to a newspaper-seller in Trafalgar Square. They sat down gratefully to smoke their home-grown pot. Many things irritated me irrationally – not what I'd expected from the heart of darkness – and we set off again as quickly as I could scramble, tripping over a vine now and again, not realising until later that I was suffering from progressive altitude sickness. We were close to 11,000 feet and all around were plants invented – one might think – by the props director of a sci-fi film.

To celebrate our arrival at Camp Two in six hours – one and a half hours under par, Jean assured me – he opened a bottle of Pernod, which, together with fresh lime juice 'for its vitamin content', somehow evaporated during what my diary records as a 'riotous night'. Jean's first concern was for his cannibals in the adjacent hut. They were given two dozen bottles of Pepsi-cola, which they enlivened with something of their own, and as much tinned meat as they could eat. Shrieks of laughter showed it was all going down pretty well.

Three cheerful Banisanza, porters renowned for their carrying ability – St Paul (Peko), Jean's personal servant; St Mark (M'waki) and St John (Yanni), two good fellows who had more than once physically supported me on the way up – looked after us at table. But first, said Jean apologetically, they had to be recanonised, all part of a ceremony they thoroughly enjoyed. Peko dutifully bowed his head and Jean broke a plate over it, leaving him with a china halo which, Jean said, he treasured although he already owned six or seven. My two candidates were also duly initiated. Of things thereafter I have no exact recollection nor record, except that we were shaken by periodical tremors and outside the hyraxes roared with a noise like the tearing of an old calico bag.

What I did know was that five of us were intent on leaving at three o'clock in the morning to climb through a forest, then up a near-vertical bed of lava, whatever the effect of Pernod.

The old tin alarm clock went off like a fire-station bell. Jean insisted I swop suede bush boots for a hobnailed pair which had gone slightly mouldy. We put on cloaks and carried torches as well as our bamboo poles. Assuring me we'd be up there and back again in just over a couple of hours (untrue), he led the way through distinctly wet tree ferns as high as the palm house at Kew. Something moist about the size of a penny alighted on my forehead. Another on my bare right arm. Bright yellow tree frogs with luminous eyes. They belched politely as I flicked them off. The place swarmed with them.

The forest thinned and ended abruptly at the foot of a hewn-out lava staircase. By looking almost directly upwards I saw the rim of fire, the outermost of the old craters. Above that, high up, thank God, horizontal

Immature giant

lightning, most of it flickery, like curtains woven from silver thread. At times there were monstrous flashes, three or four times in succession and each in the very track of the first. The sound as of static from a radio turned up *fortissimo*; the smell somewhere between boiling asphalt and sulphur.

I felt giddy, tired and slightly sick. Probably I stumbled. The palms of two strong, black sympathetic hands, those of St Mark and St John, one on each side, grasped my shoulders, firmly. Altitude sickness, not Pernod, Jean said.

We got up there and walked round for a bit, but not for very long. The heat came not from the crater immediately below us (extinct) but from an adjacent one which from a depth of just over a thousand feet spat out 'bombs' of white-hot lava. Those that overshot its rim rolled down into our safety barrier.

Two thirds of the way down, that is, just before we reached the realm of the little frogs, the fiery-coloured clouds behind us slowly faded from mauve to a lava-like grey, shot through now and again by vicious strokes of lateral lightning. 'It's going to rain like hell,' said Jean.

And it did. And I didn't care a damn. Just outside the huts about half a dozen porters had dug out a water-hole and as they knelt down to drink before breakfast in the half-light before dawn their curly heads looked like pickled walnuts.

APPROACHING PYGMY COUNTRY

Jean came out of the *gendarmerie* with the wrinkled brows of a dachshund unable to decide between breakfast and a walk in the park. He looked at the cannibals lolling about around their truck. He looked at me and said explosively, 'Sod the lot of them!'

This, from a man normally so suave, so urbane, all but told me what had happened. He'd phoned both Gaston and Donis, and learned that His Excellency had again changed his plans. In safari language, he'd shot 'the big two', elephant and buffalo, both animals that had to be culled because of overpopulation of females, but now he wanted a *bongo*.

'A what?'

'A large, beautiful, chocolate-coloured antelope, white striped as if done by hand with luminous paint. They live in thick forests, like those we saw two days ago, but you can't shoot there. *Réserve intégrale*. Totally protected despite a surplus. Another of Uncle Victor's silly ideas.'

'What's holding back that Yale glaciologist Foster Flint and his wife?'

Okapi in captivity

'New England courtesy, and, in my opinion, snobbishness, *noblesse*

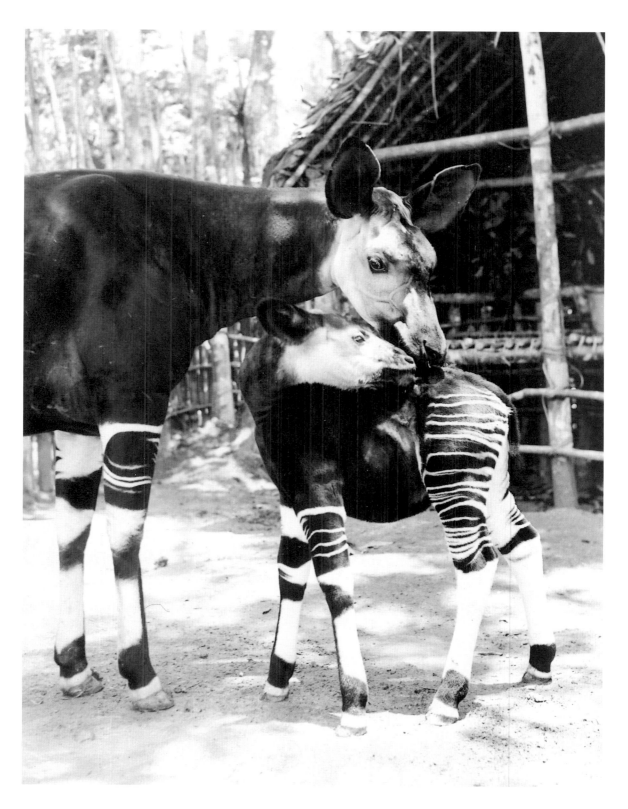

Lunar lake

Daughter of giants

oblige. He's been invited to hunt with the Governor of a colonial state and feels he ought to stick it out.'

We had arrived at Butumbo, which boasted three-star hotels, a small resident population of two or three hundred Europeans living the life of Larry with gin and Scotch at about ten bob a litre, and little to put up with except disrespectful busloads of tourists. The settlers grew coffee, quinine and pyrethrum (a big daisy and the world's safest pesticide, distinctly unpopular with Shell, ICI and the US Cyanamid Corporation).

It is where I should have been based except for a passion, difficult to explain briefly, to get on to the roof of Africa, the topmost spine of the whole continent, the Mountains of the Moon.

'So what next?'

'I've *told* Donis – I didn't ask him – to send the Flints to Kolongi, a seminary of the White Fathers, within three days. It's the first stop on our way up to the glaciers.'

After much chattering in a language I couldn't understand, the outcome was that the local Sisters of the Oblate of the Assumption would look after the cannibals for the equivalent of ten quid all in, plus their normal rations, whilst Jean and I would do what Ariel called 'embassage to the pygmies' on our own.

Pygmy drummers

The predictable outcome – though not to me at the time – bathos, anti-climax, which I suppose is another name for reality.

In his new Land Rover Jean drove fast to the Hotel Okapi, 'Heart of the land of the Forest Gypsies', a phrase which sounds better in ad-man's French. Sixty miles.

Belgium held a colonial leasehold on all the forests. Okapi is the rare, short-necked, chocolate-coloured giraffe that lives in tangled growths impenetrable to anyone except pygmies who fall-trapped them and, if the animals were uninjured, were required to deliver them to a compound run by a Portuguese vet who conditioned them to life in captivity for eventual sale, for a great deal of money, to European zoos. Too many zoos, Headquarters (Camille Donis) suspected, were in possession of undocumented specimens of *Okapia johnstonia* which has only been known since 1900, although the Little People have probably been eating them for thousands of years.

Could Jean first find out who was fixing what? Simple answer: no, although we got some names, addresses and vehicle numbers.

Before we reached the Hotel Okapi I had been reading Jean's copy

220

of Anne Eisner Putnam's book *Eight Years with Congo Pygmies* (1955) in which she wrote:

> I looked at the men, strong, happy and unspoiled by the complexities of civilisation. Then I looked at the women, so functionally female in their nakedness, so obviously pleased by their lot. There was no hypertension, no ulcer-breeding unrest here in the Ituri Forest. There was fire and there was meat and cover and love and laughter. They wanted nothing else.

When we reached the hotel there were eight large limousines, mostly American, parked outside. A six-course menu. At the back half a dozen pygmies, improbably painted up, were industriously cutting and hammering out tin-plated spears and barbed arrow-heads from the flattened sides of jerry cans.

When Jean went off to look for the vet, I selected a small bow and arrow from a great deal of crude weaponry and airport art around the pub bar. It was flimsy and cost the equivalent of about two pounds, part of a 'panoply'. I looked at it, critically, and told the little fellow I'd give him another pound if he could hit the trunk of a palm tree, in which I'd stuck a twenty-franc coin. Cautiously I stood about twenty yards to his left. He missed the tree by about two yards. Madame came out and said, apologetically, she didn't think he'd ever handled a bow before.

Room to let

Moonscapes

Jean returned with the news that the Portuguese hadn't been seen for at least a month, and as he'd taken two heavy trucks with him the chances were high that he'd done a private deal with the Little People and was operating from behind the Sudan border. Jean felt he'd better tell Donis. No reply there. Bukavu, like Brussels, closed down at half-past five.

The next morning we were on our way to the mountains early, rejoicing that at long last there was light at the end of the tunnel. The Flints had left the previous day for our rendezvous with the White Fathers. Donis didn't think Flint was fit enough to get beyond Camp Two, certainly not up to the glaciers.

'That's going to be difficult,' said Jean. 'It's just what he came out here for. For years he's had the theory that what we call the Pleistocene, the Ice Ages, were correlated with fantastic downpours, the Great Pluvials on both sides of the equator. An interesting idea. It could be that the whole river systems of the Congo and Niger were once a huge lake far bigger than the Mediterranean.'

'That explains a lot,' I said. 'It looks like that from the map, a mass of tributaries, at least in Congo. I've never seen the Niger. But tell me more about these White Fathers.'

Ever upwards

Near the top

'Excellent fellows. The finest missionaries I've ever met. There's eight or nine of them up there at Losinga led by their Father Superior, Adelbert of Oran, a French-Algerian. He's an authority on St Augustine. I mean of course Augustine of Hippo, a Berber, possibly Black. Not that tactless old fool sent to England by St Gregory the Pope to sort out your quarrelsome Christians.

'The White Fathers started in Oran about a hundred years ago. They believe in religious teaching, faith by good works, agriculture, irrigation and woodwork. Their predecessors built this seminary. Superb place. You can see for about forty miles from their balcony. The chances are that we shall have dinner up there, *al fresco*, by torch light.'

We saw the flaming cones on the top of a cliff half an hour before we chugged up there in low gear. A medieval sight. On our approach the fraternity looked like a *corps de ballet*. Cheerful, heavily bearded fellows, each one in a white tunic, and a mantle or burnous with a rosary around the neck. Betty and Richard Foster Flint were among them.

Introductions over, Jean immediately asked about his men. Father Adelbert assured him they were being looked after. Then we sat down to eat and drink liberally. The Flints were on either side of our host; I sat opposite them between Father Patrice, a stocky little fellow who spoke fluent English, and Jean who, trained at Louvain, teased the whole company, mischievously, always politely, quoting Voltaire and Nietzsche on celibacy and sobriety, in a way they all clearly enjoyed, leaving the last word to their Superior only rarely when they were unable to answer for themselves.

I recall Adelbert saying that few women were ever really pious until the age of forty, and then except on deeply philosophical subjects they tended to be somewhat banal. As for drink, the Fathers never touched anything alcoholic except when they had visitors; that's why they always made such a fuss of them. Much of this went over my head. My eyes were on their bronzed faces, their expressions redoubled in intensity in the flickering light of those huge torches, and my ears on the orchestrated talk of intellectuals heard above the incessant noises of the jungle from the velvety dark all around us.

Jean spoke to me briefly, privately, the next day. Flint suffered from blood pressure and some minor heart complaint, but he wasn't as bad as Donis had made out. As Jean saw it, he'd better split the party up. I should go ahead with Father Pat and most of the cannibals to prepare and stock up the next hut, and he'd follow on slowly. I'd be safe with Pat. He was not only an alpinist but had climbed most of the peaks in the Ruwenzori.

'Climbed! Have we any climbing to do?'

'Only at one point. *Le cable*. After all, you've been over the proving ground, Nyiragongo. You'll be able to do it with one hand.'

'Why are we trudging along with armed guards? They don't do any work.'

'Up there among the *Eruyère arborescence* there are some fierce beasts. We don't want to phone your Uncle Victor to ask him to tell the *New*

York Times that their Congolese correspondent is, regretfully, as far as we know, inside the digestive tract of an aggressive specimen of *Panthera pardus Ruwenzori*, the giant leopard.' Jean, as I've mentioned before, had a dry sense of humour.

At eight o'clock he set off with the Flints, leaving me with Father Pat, who celebrated Mass with our retinue kneeling down in the wet grass – '*Baba yetu*' (Our Father) – before loading themselves with immense head burdens, including a tied up but still live Muscovy duck which squawked miserably for two days until it was killed for our celebratory dinner. Long before then I wished it could escape or that someone would wring its neck.

Our course, steeper by far than the others', lay through giant ferns, bamboo and those abominable heathers. At their feet lay bright green tropical moss, such as Jean had warned me against on Nyiragongo. Pat told me some of it was deep enough to engulf elephants.

Were they, I wondered, the small species *cyclotis* with round ears peculiar to the Congo? (Like Bertie, but smaller.) He nodded. They were quite common up to 12,000 feet and until they were a year or two

Last day but one

226

Roof of Africa

old they were covered in thick red hair. They looked like miniature mammoths in the snow.

With his knowledge of anthropology and natural history Pat could scarcely have been a more informative companion.

'Why does Jean refer to his porters as cannibals?' I asked.

He smiled. Among them were descendants of eastern tribes of the Banande and Bakonjo who, some early missionaries reported, had what he called 'some deplorable habits'.

Early settlers had told him how they had been known to eat their next-door neighbours' senile relations and, in return, they sold them their own infirm. 'Could not this be called primitive economy?' They didn't buy slaves and fatten them up like the Middle Congo tribes. They were a relatively peaceful people: no slaves; no prisoners of war; no cemeteries. In Ki-n'wana, the language of the river, he said they were called 'yam-yams'. Basic stuff related by a practical priest.

At the next hut he promptly got the men to work under my two ever-helpful companions, St Mark and St John, for what he called a *nettoyage général*, a thorough clean-up. They peered into every crack and crevice, even under the floorboards and thatched eaves, for snakes, centipedes and scorpions, and then swept the place out. This done, Pat went out to ensure that the men had more than enough food and were comfortable under their own lean-to, where they had lit – I don't know how – a fire. He came back to read in his office for the day while I wrote up my notes.

Half-past six. Almost dark and no sign of the others. He sensed my concern and said reassuringly he could guess what had happened. Jean had taken them up to a hut in an adjacent valley far less steep but less spectacular than ours. Not far from there Foster Flint could examine large glacial remains which would tell him, he imagined, all that he wanted to know with less physical exertion than climbing any further.

Pat looked at me. 'Perhaps,' he suggested, 'a small drink might be a good thing for prophylactic purposes. Altitude sickness can be very enervating and we have a stiff climb ahead of us.' I helped myself to a large one.

All turned out as he predicted. Before we took to our bunks the Blessed St Paul, Jean's personal servant, arrived with a note that said he was keeping an eye on the Flints for a couple of days. They were distinctly unwell, and he hoped to rejoin us on the way down.

For myself I felt self-confident in this strange and magical world, but the next day showed I still had a great deal to learn.

The sky at first light was marked only by what alpinists call *alpenglow*. Dawn broke. Clouds as delicate as the tails of egrets glowed and caught fire on the summits of the Stanley group; Margherita, Alexandra, Albert, Moebius, Elena and Savoia, all around the 16,000–17,000 feet mark. With their white walls and rose-coloured roof, the components of the great massif looked like the pavilions of a chief among the tents of his men; from where I stood, shivering slightly as I peered through our door, the greatest of them was Margherita.

With nothing better to do in the half-light, I stepped out wearing one thick cape and carrying another in addition to my bamboo pole. A stroll, I felt, might be in order. Perhaps I could collect a few insects. Among those grotesque heathers I spread the second cape on the ground and began to beat the lower branches. Standard technique. Down fell a few weevils. Entirely new species, as it later turned out, but not the by-product of capturing them.

A screech from something, probably a hyrax, I thought, then a heavy, throat-clearing cough. I looked up. An immense, curiously white-looking leopard was looking down on me from halfway up the tree.

I've forgotten what I felt or what I did, except stay put with my staff upraised. The leopard coughed again, bared its teeth and leaped into the next tree. By that time I recall only walking backwards towards the hut, shouting and waving my staff. Pat, in his charitable fashion, was only mildly reproachful.

The second incident occurred within three hours of leaving the hut. It entailed climbing through an overgrown track which can't have been used for months. Isolated trees overhung with moss and lianas. Mark and John went ahead with *pangas*, slapping their buttocks and pointing at anything untoward. Then a narrow ledge alongside a wall of rock. It ended, as far as I could make out, in a void, an emptiness, nothing visible beyond, not even on the horizon.

Pat took the lead. He walked about fifty yards, stopped, looked up, peered over the edge, then beckoned me on.

A heavy rope about an inch thick hung in loops from some substantial rivets and then disappeared behind the invisible side of an arête. There were not even toe-holds below the rope.

'This,' Pat said in a nonchalant voice, 'is *le cable*. Far easier than it looks.' I gazed at it in dismay

Mark and John took to the cable with the alacrity of children on a swing. They went round twice with their burdens tied to their waists. Pat followed them, and then came back to reassure me. '*C'est facile, non?*'

I smiled, bleakly, and took off with an assumed air of nonchalance, not daring to look down.

Two pairs of warm black hands grasped my shoulders on the far side. I could have embraced these good companions. It was, I think, the most physically daring thing I had ever done. For perhaps ten or fifteen seconds I had no support except my half-outstretched arms.

A mountaineer friend to whom I later related this said that it was near the bottom of the alpine scale of intrepidity from one to ten. But no more for me. And the spectre of that blasted cable on the return trip haunted my thoughts throughout that day of giant vegetables, glaciers, vultures and elephants in the snow.

Below us the landscape had changed as if in the last grand transformation scene of an opera. Pat handed me his field glasses. Like all transitions of vegetation on Ruwenzori, it was abrupt. I had become familiar with giant grasses, bamboos, heathers and wild bananas, which Pat described as 'plants which have never done anything about it'. They bore no visible fruit. The few trees were twisted into weird shapes and gnarled, so that they resembled a drawing by Arthur Rackham. Out of each trunk glared a face, sometimes benign, but more often wicked and bearded with motionless streamers of lichens and mosses.

From the floor of that small valley the glaciers arose to the summit of Margherita, so blindingly white that when the fitful sun caught them we were obliged to put on darkened glasses, almost of the kind used by welders.

Another transition. Between the bearded trees and the ice were bogs and small lakes that reeked of hydrogen sulphide, smashed vegetation reduced to glacier melt. On the slightly drier ground were vaguely familiar plants which seemed to have been injected with overdoses of growth hormones; different-coloured lobelias and yellow daisy-like ragworts (*Senecio*) up to thirty feet in height. We felt dwarfed.

Lest this sounds an exaggeration I shall quote a distinguished botan-

Source of the Nile

230

ist and professional plant hunter, Patrick M. Synge, for years the editor of the Royal Horticultural Society's *Journal*.

A grey mist made a fitting background to the most monstrous and unearthly landscape that I have ever seen. Vague outlines of peaks and precipices towered around us. Here were plants which seemed more like ghosts of past ages than ordinary trees and herbs. They appeared as a weird and terrible dream to me, a botanist and hunter of strange plants. It all seemed unreal, like some imaginary reconstruction of life in a long-past geological age, or even upon another planet. Our own familiar common herbs seemed to have gone mad. Although not lunar in fact they well lived up to that name in appearance. On the ground grew a thick carpet of mosses, some very brilliant yellow, others deep crimson in colour. Every shade of green was represented and the tree trunks were also clothed in thick moss, often tussocked into the semblance of faces. It is good to be able to escape sometimes from the ordinary world; this strange mountain carried us into a dreamland which was often a fairy-land, occasionally a nightmare.*

We crunched up a strip of glacier about half a mile wide. The canni-bals were reluctant to climb up into what couldn't easily be seen. Father Pat gave them a handful of cigarettes and a ten-minute break before he shouted, '*Kwenda, Kwenda tagende* (Get up and put your loads on your heads).'

It was not only bare and white but mysterious, unearthly. There was no sound except our footfalls and distant falling water – *Ruwenzu*, in an ancient African language. Here the silence became the voice. It seemed to present a challenge to the man who invaded its solitude; the mountain appeared antagonistic and tried to frighten him back again with its uncanny aspects, its cold, its dampness, its otherworldliness.

A slowly descending mist from a height of about 15,000 feet finally drove us back. Father Pat looked at it through his glasses. He shook his head slowly and said, '*Ito m'baya sana na hatari* – not only bad, but dangerous.'

He looked again at a far distant strip of green to our left, perhaps a couple of hundred feet below us. We were not alone on Margherita, and we were not the only creatures intent on retreating. He smiled and passed the glasses to me.

Presumably after a midday lunch on young lobelia shoots, a dozen or more small elephants with their red-haired *totos* between them were ambling down to the safety of the valley, with dignity.

* *In Search of Flowers* Patrick M. Synge. (Michael Joseph 1973)

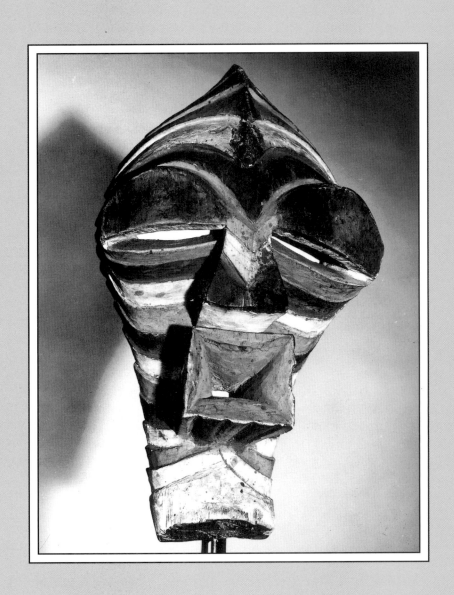

Acknowledgements and Picture Credits

The author and publisher would like to thank the following for permission to reproduce illustrations:

Hugh Miles for caribou pictures on pages 26 and 27

The Trustees of the British Museum for the illustrations of masks on pages 36, 43, 47 and 232

Andrew Hill and the Hutchinson library for pictures of the Congo on pages 38, 42, 46, 50 and 55

Ed van der Elsken: Abelard Shuman for the photograph of the elephant hunter on page 56

Micheal Stead for photographs of moorland on pages 159 and 166

Derrick Champion for his family photographs on page 169

Guy Yeoman for Ruwenzori illustrations on pages 182, 190, 195, 207, 210, 215, 218, 219, 222, 223, 224, 227, 230

L M McGowan for the giant heather photograph on page 203

Other photographs are the author's.

The epigraph is from Tennyson's *Ulysses*.

Finally, the author and the publisher wish to record their gratitude for the generosity of Constable and Co. Ltd., for permission to reprint extracts which were first published by them in John Hillaby's previous books.

233

INDEX

Aboud (syce), 122, 126
Achnashellach (Scotland), 88
Adamson, George, 209
Adalbert of Oran, Father, 224–5
Agar, Mrs (of North Yorkshire), 154
Algonquin Park (Canada), 11–13
Altnaharra Hotel (Scotland), 94
Anselm, St, 65
ants, 54, 189, 191
arctic fox, 21
arctic lynx, 25
Armadale family and Bible (N. Yorkshire), 156–7
Arusha (Tanzania), 99
Assynt (Scotland), 84
Athabasca, Lake (Canada), 14, 20
Athabascan group (languages), 21

Babali people (Congo), 45
Backhaus, Dieter, 49
Balharry, Dick, 88
Balquidder (Scotland), 81
Barrens, The (Canada), 9, 22
Bastien, Marie, 14–15
Bata Shoe Corporation, 37, 39
Benn Eighe Nature Reserve (Scotland), 88
Betsy (prostitute, Uranium City), 16–17
Bettyhill (Scotland), 94, 96
Black Mountains (Gwent), 60
Boorstin, Daniel, 10
Borders, Scottish, 76–80
Borlase, Copeland, 64
Botallack (Cornwall), 64
Breadalbane (Bridalbin; Scotland), 82
Bristol, 60
Bruyères, Camp des (Congo), 207
Buccleuch family, 77
Buckland, William, 197

Bukavu (Congo), 48–9, 51, 187, 189
Butombo (Congo), 218

cairns, 64
Caithness, Sinclair, Earl of, 77
Callander (Scotland), 81
camels, 100, 101–2, 104, 106, 108–9, 111–14, 117, 122, 124, 126, 132
Campbell, Sir John, 82
cannibalism, 228
Caporali (pygmy; 'Little Corporal'), 202
Carbis Bay (Cornwall), 66
caribou, 222, 229
Carn Gluze (Cornwall), 64
Carn Kenidjack (Cornwall), 64
Carrigill (Pennines), 76
Cassian, John, 142
Champion, Arthur, 162–3, 167–8, 170
Chapin, Jim, 187, 193, 197, 200–2, 204
Chapin, Ruth, 201, 204
Cheviot Hills, 76
Chicken, Louis, 25–7, 29, 33
chimpanzees, 212
Chipewyan Indians, 21–2
Chual Aluinn (waterfall; Scotland), 93
Churchill, Sir Winston, 181
Civil, Alan, 20
Congo (river and region), 37–57, 183–231
Conrad, Joseph, 12
Cornwall, 64–6
Couverte, Madame (of Hôtel Ishango), 196–7
Covananters (Presbyterian), 76–7
Cree Indians, 24, 32
crocodiles, 54, 197–8
Crosland, Richard, 156
Crow, Germain, 26

Dartmoor, 66–9
Dean, Forest of, 60
Dedoth people (Uganda), 101
deer, red, 85–6
Deirdre (Celtic heroine), 65
de Lacy, William and Hugh, 69
Derbyshire, 72–3
Dessary, Glen (Scotland), 84
Dixon, Willie, 152, 154
Dj'amm El F'naa (Marrakesh), 173, 176
Dochart, Glen (Scotland), 81–2
Dogrib Indians, 31–2
Donis, Camille, 41, 49, 57, 187, 189, 191,
    193, 209, 216, 218, 220, 222, 225
Donis, Celestine, 49–51
Dounreay (Scotland), 96
dress and footware, 61, 133
drove roads (Scotland), 60
drums and drumming (Africa), 45, 48,
    184–5
Duncansby Head (Scotland), 97
Duwarmish Indians, 33

eagles, 85
Edale (Pennine Way), 73
Edward, Lake (Africa), 194, 196–7
Einstein, Albert, 19
Eldorado UC5 (mine, Canada), 16,
    18–19
elephants, 112, 123–4, 198–201, 209,
    212, 227

Farndale (N. Yorkshire), 152, 154, 164
Figaro (servant, Stanleyville), 41
Finiskaig (Scotland), 83
Flint, Betty, 225
Flint, Professor Richard Foster, 49, 57,
    216, 218, 222, 225, 228
footware see dress and footware
Fort Rae (Canada), 31
Fort William (Scotland), 82

Garthwaite, Kitty, 152, 154–7
giraffes, 126
Glaoui, Madami and T'hami, 176–7, 180
Glencoe (Scotland), 82
Glencoul (Scotland), 93
Goiti (camel driver), 129, 132
Goli (Congolese cook), 209–10
Goose Bay (Canada), 9–10
gorillas, 53
Grant's gazelles, 114–15, 123, 187

Great Bear Lake (Canada), 29, 31
Greene, Graham, 12
Guillaume, Général Augustine, 173,
    180–1

Hare Indians, 32
Harry (Canadian odd-job man), 31–2
Hassan, King of Morocco, 177
heather, 148, 151–2
Hebden Bridge Times, 73
Heinzelin, Jean de, 51, 53, 57, 187, 197,
    201–2, 204–10, 212, 214, 216, 218,
    220–2, 225–6, 228–9
Herskovitz, M. J., 49, 57
hippopotami, 192
hobs (hobgoblins), 164, 167
Hohnel, Ludwig von, 132
Honddu Valley (Wales), 69
honey-guides (birds), 202, 204
Hudson Bay, 9, 24
huskies (dogs), 19–20
Hutton-le-Hole (N. Yorkshire): Folk
    Museum, 156
Hutu people, 184
hyenas, 125–6
hyraxes, 209, 214, 229

Ia, St, 65
Ikky, Indolent (Turkana fisherman),
    136–7, 139–43
Inchnadamph, 89, 91
Indian Agency (Canada), 21–2, 32–3
Indians, North American (Redmen),
    21–35
Ishango (Congo), 196–8
Ituri river (Congo), 48, 189

Jade Sea see Rudolf, Lake
Jake (Canadian ranger), 13
Jedburgh (Scotland), 80
John o'Groats (Scotland), 96–7
Johnston family (Scottish Borders), 77
Jouvet, Louis, 204

Kagera Park (Congo), 53
Karo (Samburu syce), 103, 106, 109,
    112, 114–15, 117, 120, 122–3, 126,
    133, 136, 143, 145
Khartoum, 40
Kigali (Zaire), 184
Kilvert, Revd Francis, 66
Kinder Scout (Derbyshire), 73

Kingwana language, 47
Kirton Glen (Scotland), 81
Kitiwala (African independence
    movement), 40, 48
Kivu (Congo), 41, 48
Kivu, Lake (Congo), 39, 48, 193
Kulal, Mount (Kenya), 132, 136

Laban, Pierre, 26
Land's End (England), 59–61, 65
Larsen, Inga, 18
Larsen, Kurt, 14, 17, 19, 21
Lastingham (N. Yorkshire), 154, 156
Laurentides National Park, Quebec, 13
Lawson, Don, 13
Lelean (African headman), 108–9,
    112–17, 120, 122–3, 126, 129, 133,
    136–7, 139–40, 143, 145
lemmings, 21
Lenduroni (African), 122–4
Lengama (African), 124, 137
Leo, Father, 21, 25, 29
leopards, 209–10, 229
Leopold, Aldo, 198
Lévy-Bruhl, Lucien, 53
Llanthony Priory (Wales), 69
Lokele people (Congo), 45, 48, 185
London, Jack: *Call of the Wild*, 12
Longippi Hills (Kenya), 140
Louna ford (Farndale, N. Yorkshire),
    152, 154
Luib (Scotland), 82
lycaons (Cape hunting dogs), 136–7
Lyke Wake (N. Yorkshire), 157–60
lynx *see* arctic lynx

McClean, Larry, 15, 18
McDougal, Doc, 17
Mackenzie river (Canada), 31
McReady ('Mercredi'), Jock, 19–21,
    24–7, 29
Malaya (Samburu prostitute), 118, 120
mambas (snakes), 52–3
Margherita (mountain, Ruwenzori),
    229–30
Marrakesh (Morocco), 173, 176
masks (Africa), 53
Matthews range (Kenya), 109
Maxwell family (Scottish Borders), 77
Maxwell, Gavin, 173, 177, 181
Megalithic culture, 64
'Men of the North' (BBC series), 20

Mercredi, Jock *see* McReady, Jock
Mezek (Turkana cook), 113, 123, 133,
    136–7, 139, 141–3, 145
Micha, Marc, 54
Micklethwaite, Ned, 162–3, 167
mining: Canada, 16–19; North
    Yorkshire, 168, 170
missionaries: in Africa, 53–4
Mohammed V, King of Morocco, 177
Morar, Loch (Scotland), 84
Morocco, 173–81
Morse, Samuel, 45
mosquitoes, 16–18
Moulay Hassan, Sultan, 177, 180
mourning dove, 210
Munta (camel driver), 111–12, 117
Mutara, Charlie, 42, 44–5
M'waki ('St Mark'; porter), 214, 216,
    228–9

Nairobi (Kenya), 101–2
Napier, Alexander, 76
Napoleon I (Bonaparte), Emperor, 158
National Albert park (Congo), 49
N'doto Hills (Kenya), 124, 126
Neumann, Arthur H., 140
Nevis, Ben, 83
Nevis, Loch, 84
New York Times, 19
Northumberland, 76
North Yorkshire National Park, 148
No-see-ums (black flies), 17
Nova Scotia, 10
Nyiragongo (volcano; Ruwenzori), 53,
    57, 204–6, 225

okapi, 220
Ol Conto pass (Kenya), 109, 111
Ory, Maurice, 48
OTRACO (Office d'exploitation des
    Transports Coloniaux), 41
Ottawa, 12

Pango (manservant), 51–2, 54, 57, 183,
    186–8
Patrice, Father, 225–6, 228–31
Pavel, Peter, 37, 39–41, 42, 48
peacocks: in Africa, 204
Pearson, Lester, 13
Peebles (Scotland), 30
Peko ('St Paul'; porter), 214, 228
Pennine Way, 60

pitchblende, 18
Potteries, The (England), 69–72
Putnam, Eisner: *Eight Years with Congo Pygmies*, 221
pygmies, 202, 218, 220–1

quoits, 64

red deer, 85–6
Redouté, Pierre Joseph, 192, 197
rhinoceros, 52, 54
Roberts, Father, 158
rock pythons, 54
Rodosoit (Kenya), 120, 122
Rudolf, Lake ('the Jade Sea'), 99–101, 132, 140, 142–3, 145
Ruwenzori, 51, 54, 57, 191, 196, 230–1
Ryedale (N. Yorkshire), 148, 160

St Ives (Cornwall), 65–6
Samburu people (East Africa), 103, 113–14, 117, 124, 129
Scotland, 76, 80–7
Scottish thistle, 9–10
Sealth, Chief of the Duwarmish, 33, 35
Semliki river (Congo), 197
Shin, Loch (Scotland), 93
Silpho Moor (N. Yorkshire), 157–8
snakes, 52–4, 184
South Horr (Kenya), 126, 129
Spenthorpe, Alf, 158
Sroine (mountain, Scotland), 82
Stanley, (Sir) Henry Morton, 45, 205
Stanleyville (*later* Kisangani), 41
Stoke-on-Trent, 69, 72
stone circles, 64–5
Stonehenge, 64
Stony Rapids (Canada), 21, 24
Straelen, Professor Victor van ('Uncle Victor'), 50, 187, 189, 201, 207, 216, 225
Sutherland, Earls of (Gordon family), 10
Synge, Patrick M.: *In Search of Flowers*, 231

Talavera, Battle of (1809), 157
Teleki von Sek, Count, 132, 142
Telouet (Morocco), 176–7, 180–1

Thesiger, Wilfred, 100, 102, 133, 140
Thorfinn the Mighty, Earl, 96
Thorgill (N. Yorkshire), 148, 162, 168
Trent and Mersey Canal, 69
Tuareg people, 173
Turkana people (Uganda), 101, 136–7, 139–41

Ullapool (Scotland), 88
uranite, 18
uranium, 18–19
Uranium City (Canada), 13–16
Ussher, James, Archbishop of Armagh, 197

Valentine, Vic, 20–2, 29
volcanoes: Africa, 205–6, 214, 216

Wagenia people (Congo), 44–5
Wainwright, Job, 158
Wamba (Kenya), 99–103, 106
warthogs, 183, 186, 189, 191–3
waterbuck, 209
Watusi people, 184
Wellington, Arthur Wellesley, 1st Duke of, 157
Wetherill, George, 162
whippoorwill (bird), 13–14
White Fathers (missionaries), 222, 224–5
Wistman's Wood (Devon), 68
Witte, Baron Gaston de, 51–4, 57, 99, 183–7, 189, 191, 197, 200–1, 216
wolverines (gluttons), 24
wolves, 13–14, 19–21, 29
wood buffaloes, 17
Woon Gumpus Common (Cornwall), 64
World Wildlife Fund, 99
Wrath, Cape (Scotland), 96
Wren, P. C.: *Beau Geste*, 173
Wye Valley, 60

Yanni ('St John'; porter), 214, 216, 228
Yohanni (Somali), 191, 193–4, 196–7, 200
Yorkshire, 73, 147–71

Zouhir the Scholar, 176–7